K9

Reviews

I enjoyed reading this book. It provides a lot of useful information to officers. Officers are often instructed about use of force, but not about what that means in a practical sense or what civil litigation entails. This book addresses readers in a more informal way, officer to officer, rather than sounding too "lawyerly."
— *Taylor S. Rahn,*
Robles, Rael & Anaya, P.C. ABQ, NM

[*K9s In the Courtroom* brings the authors'] years of experience as law-enforcement canine professionals to bear on the liability risks facing every department that operates a canine unit. The authors do an excellent job of identifying the areas of concern that each handler and supervisor must understand to survive in the jungle known as the civil justice system.
— *John M. Peters, PLC,*
Attorney in MI

Lawsuits happen, and most bites will result in litigation where lawyers will crawl all over your agency's training program and canine deployment history. [The authors provide] thorough and timely advice from a wealth of practical experience, primarily as handlers and teachers, but also as police procedures expert witnesses. *K9s In the Courtroom* is an essential read for every handler, canine supervisor, and risk manager. These tips will lessen the blow of civil litigation, help guide you through it, and may prevent it from happening in the first place."
— *Timothy J. Kral, Esq.*
Police Defense Attorney
Manning Kass & Ramirez, Los Angeles, CA

K9s In the Courtroom

BRAD SMITH • JEFF BARRETT • ANDREW B. WEIMAN • TED DAUS

Eggleston, Virginia

Copyright © 2015 by Brad Smith, Jeff Barrett, Andrew B. Weiman, Ted Daus

All rights reserved. No part of this book may be reproduced or transmitted in any form or by any means, electronic or mechanical, including photocopying, recording, or any information storage and retrieval system, without permission in writing from the authors, except in the case of a brief quotation in critical reviews.

Published by Wolfe Media Resources

Printed in the United States of America

Edited by Joanne Wolfe, Wolfe Media Resources
Designed by Marisa Dirks, M Design
On the cover: K9 Arlo
Front cover photograph courtesy of K9 Officer Dale Merchant and K9 Arlo, Garfield Heights (OH) Police Department

ISBN 978-0-692-35963-1

Table of Contents

	Dedication	11
	Authors	12
	Acknowledgments	16
	Preface	18
Chapter 1:	**Civil Litigation — Outrageous Payouts**	**21**
Chapter 2:	**Bulletproof Your K9 Unit**	**23**
	A "textbook" deployment?	23
	The realities of civil litigation	25
	The good, the bad, and the ugly	27
	Decreasing liability due to accidental bites	32
	The bottom line	33
Chapter 3:	**Creating a Successful K9 Unit**	**34**
	Selecting a vendor and trainer	35
	K9 policy	38
	Selecting a K9 handler	40
	Selecting a police dog	42
	Decoys	44
	K9 supervision	45
Chapter 4:	**Training to Avoid Liability**	**48**
	Field training officer programs	48
	Dealing effectively with accidental bites	48
	K9 settlement agreement	49
	Maintenance training	50
	Advanced K9 training is critical	51
	Recordkeeping	54
	Unit assessment	55
	Briefing and in-service training	56

Table of Contents

(Chapter 4 continued):
- Training for the street..................................57
- Overwhelming force....................................59
- Non-compliant or passive suspects..................60
- Call-off and re-direct..................................61
- Don't be afraid to fail in training.....................61

Chapter 5:   Avoiding K9 Deployment Errors................62
- Foot pursuit or perimeter?............................62
- Danger for backup officers...........................62
- Making the wise move.................................63
- Stop and evaluate......................................63
- K9 deployment...65
- Other force options....................................67
- Control the rush..68
- Know your limitations.................................69
- Who is in charge of the search team?..............69
- Pre-deployment briefings and assignments.........70
- Safety equipment......................................72
- Staging the heroes: paramedics on-scene..........73
- K9 bite pictures..74
- Debriefing the incident................................76

Chapter 6:   K9 Announcements..............................77
- Where to give your K9 announcement..............77
- Secondary K9 announcements.......................79
- Mobile K9 announcements............................80
- What the courts say about K9 announcements....81
- What should your K9 announcements say?.........82
- Don't be in a hurry to deploy
  after your K9 announcements.....................83

Chapter 7:   Report Writing..................................85
- What you need to know before you
  write your report....................................85
- Justifying your use of force...........................85
- Post-deployment follow-up............................87
- Sample K9 bite report 88

Table of Contents

Chapter 8: **FLSA K9 Care and Maintenance**.................93
  Fair Labor Standards Act...............................93
  United States Department of Labor....................93
  Case law..94

Chapter 9: **Preparing for a Lawsuit** 96
  *What handlers can expect to be questioned
    about in court* 96
  Get to know your attorney............................ 97
  Interrogatories...99
  Request for production.................................100
  Depositions..100
  The courtroom..104

Chapter 10: **Keeping a K9 Unit Running Smoothly**...........107
  Still productive or burned out?........................107
  Stay or leave?..109
  Pressures handlers face 110
  How to recognize K9 burnout........................111
  Supervisor responsibility................................112

Chapter 11: **K9 Tracking — This Book Should Change
  Your K9 Life**..115
  Proving your worth...................................... 115
  K9 terminology...116
  Does the beginning define the end?...................117
  *Your K9 records show that you encourage
    bad behavior*..118
  *The spontaneous bite at the end
    of your tracks*...120
  *Transitioning from one phase of training
    to the next*..121
  Broadening your capabilities........................123
  Angles of attack...125
  *Aberrance could make you better, but it also
    could make you a legal target*...................127
  *Scenario-based training: the centerpiece
    of success and survival*...........................129
  *Final thoughts on the most dangerous job
    in law enforcement*................................131

Table of Contents

Chapter 12: **Detection Canine Recordkeeping................132**
Are written records needed?...........................133
Subpoena requests and requirements...............135

Chapter 13: **Dog Reliability.......................................142**
Florida v. Harris..142
Harris eliminates the misnomer "false alert"..........143
The defense attack.......................................144
Cases after Harris..145

Chapter 14: **Dogs Sniffing Houses and Apartments..........147**
Florida v. Jardines..147
Apartment use after Jardines..........................148
Another federal court ruling............................150
State Supreme Court and Jardines....................152

Chapter 15: **Checkpoints: What to Do or What Not to Do....153**
Real checkpoints..153
Fake checkpoints...155

Chapter 16: **Dogs Jumping Into Cars.........................158**
No aiding the dog...159
No handler encouragement.............................159
Change in behavior.......................................160
Search the car as you find it...........................161
Additional federal and state cases 162

Chapter 17: **Money Forfeiture and Contamination Theory...163**
Forfeiture scenarios......................................164
Discrediting global contamination theory............167

Chapter 18: **Checking Parcels for Home Delivery............170**
State court rulings..170
Federal court rulings.....................................173

Chapter 19: **Warehouses, Storage Units
and Commercial Property.......................176**
Warehouse or storage unit.............................176
Commercial property....................................180

Table of Contents

Chapter 20: Legal Issues in Using Gun Dogs..................183
    Gun searches and probable cause....................183
    Article searches..183
    Using a gun dog when executing
        a search warrant....................................185
    Gang or homicide search warrants...................186
    Consent searches...187
    Probation and parole sweeps.........................188
    School searches..188

Chapter 21: Basic Testimony 101.............................190
    Odor, not drugs...190
    Sniff, search, or scan....................................191
    Courtroom demonstrations............................191
    Dead scent, stale or lingering odor....................192
    Train on all odors..194
    False alert...194
    Canine mistakes..195
    Proofing..195

Chapter 22: Courtroom Testimony...........................197
    Discrediting testimony..................................197
    The history of Clever Hans............................ 202
    Cuing test.. 203
    Where does cuing come from?...................... 206

Index...214

K9s In the Courtroom

Dedication

MY PREVIOUS BOOK, *K9 Tactical Operations for Patrol and SWAT,* was dedicated to SWAT officers, K9 handlers, and police dogs that gave their lives in the line of duty. Sadly, since that publication, more have fallen. We honor their memory and ensure their legacy by how we continue to serve. The successful publication of this book is no different.

K9 Koda
Leon County, FL
KIA 1-31-13
■ ■ ■

K9 Kody
St. Paul, MN
KIA 2-12-13
■ ■ ■

K9 Ape
FBI HRT/K9 unit
KIA 3-14-13
■ ■ ■

K9 Ronin
Glendale PD, AZ
KIA 6-20-13
■ ■ ■

SWAT Officer Bobby Hornsby
Killeen PD, TX
KIA 7-14-13
■ ■ ■

K9 Kilo
Indiana State Police, IN
KIA 6-24-13
■ ■ ■

K9 Quanto
Edmonton PS, Canada
KIA 10-27-13
■ ■ ■

K9 Gorky
Davie County, NC
KIA 1-23-14
■ ■ ■

K9 Rocco
Pittsburgh PD, PA
KIA 1-30-14
■ ■ ■

Officer Jason Crisp and K9 Maros
Burke County, NC
KIA 3-12-14
■ ■ ■

K9 Mick
Portland PD, OR
KIA 4-16-14
■ ■ ■

Detective Charles Dinwiddie
Killeen PD, TX
KIA 5-11-14
■ ■ ■

K9 Tanja
Walker County SD, GA
KIA 6-13-14
■ ■ ■

K9 Tracker
Alabama Department of Corrections
KIA 7-14-14
■ ■ ■

K9 Kye
Oklahoma City PD, OK
KIA 8-25-14
■ ■ ■

K9 Baron
St. Johns County SD, FL
KIA 10-7-14
■ ■ ■

Authors

Brad Smith

Brad Smith is retired from the West Covina Police Department in southern California after 30 years of service. Brad was a handler and trainer for West Covina for 25 years and a SWAT dog handler for 18 years. Since 1999, Brad has been National K9 Chairman for the National Tactical Officers Association (NTOA) and a K9 Subject Matter Expert for the California Association of Tactical Officers. Brad specializes in field tactics and officer safety. He designed and implemented a K9 SWAT & K9 Patrol Tactical School called SKIDDS and CATS (www.SKIDDS.com). Brad is the owner of Canine Tactical Operations and Consulting (www.K9TacOps.com) and the author of *K9 Tactical Operations for Patrol and SWAT* and coauthor of *K9s In the Courtroom*.

Authors

Jeff Barrett

As a professional educator of adults in the law-enforcement K9 industry, Jeff Barrett has become one of the most recognized leaders for developing today's modern curriculum for advanced K9 training. Through the co-creation of the Handler Instruction & Training Seminars (HITS), and HITS Training & Consulting, Jeff and the HITS partners have created the largest law-enforcement K9 resource under one roof. Jeff and the HITS team have redefined how police K9 training and handler education are made available in the United States.

With 27-plus years of K9 handling experience, Jeff delivers his experiences and professional expert opinions throughout his contributions to this book. With a special focus on tracking, Jeff highlights the dangerous path through the courtroom and demonstrates the need for higher education, better training, and clarity of recordkeeping for K9 handlers.

Currently, Jeff is a police officer with more than 28 years on the street, and is in his 27th year as a K9 handler. Jeff's influence and leadership of the K9 industry has its solid foundation set upon his years of education, his decades of street experience, and the thousands of hours he's spent training and handling police dogs in advanced training seminars.

Jeff also takes an active role as a vice-president with USPCA's National Executive Board and sits as NTOA's vice-chairman. Jeff's professional opinions on K9 training have been published for many years in law-enforcement publications, which have reached and helped readers worldwide. Spreading the educational word helps everyone succeed, and Jeff has dedicated his career to the advancement of law-enforcement professionals though education.

Ted Daus

Ted Daus is an assistant state attorney with the Broward County State Attorney's Office in Fort Lauderdale, Florida. He has been a prosecutor for the past 23 years, the last 18 of which he has been assigned to the Drug Trafficking Unit for the State Attorney's Office. Ted was graduated from Nova Southeastern School of Law in 1991. He has extensive experience as a lecturer on search and seizure for DEA, U.S. Customs, various Florida Police Departments, the Florida Prosecuting Attorney's Association, the Police K-9 Training Institute, Police Canine Consultants, and the Canine Development Group. He lectures regularly across the country to national canine organizations such as USPCA, NPCA, and NAPWDA. He is an adjunct professor of law for Nova Southeastern University, teaching Trial Advocacy and coaching national mock trial teams. He was a legal editor and writer for *Police K-9 Magazine* for seven years. He also lectures annually at HITS, the nation's largest police canine conference, and is a partner in HITS Training & Consulting. He is the current nationwide legal advisor for the National Police Canine Association. Most recently, Ted was counsel of record for both of the following United States Supreme Court K9 cases: *Harris* and *Jardines,* argued before the court on October 31, 2012.

Authors

Andrew B. Weiman

With more than 26 years of police experience involving various assignments in a specialty drug investigation unit in South Florida, Detective Andy Weiman has become a leading expert in the field. Having nearly 20 years of K9 experience since training his first drug dog with Canadian Customs, Andy has gone on to oversee the training of a variety of detector dogs, including teams that can find drugs, currency, and firearms.

Andy's education and experience with police dog training steered his career path into developing an industry-leading recordkeeping software program called PACKTRACK®. His depth of knowledge and understanding of state and federal laws regarding search and seizure has been an enormous asset to hundreds of K9 handlers who attend his K9 training courses. Andy has served on *Police K-9 Magazine*'s Editorial Advisory Board, and has helped create Handler Instruction & Training Seminars (HITS), the training conference known for its breadth of diversified K9 training lectures, and HITS Training & Consulting.

Andy's expert opinions on drug dogs and recordkeeping in this book will help bring the entire law-enforcement K9 industry to a higher level of clarity. His countless court appearances and proven skills as an expert witness on the stand are clear testimony to the effectiveness of proper K9 recordkeeping as a means to establishing K9 reliability. As a K9 trainer and handler with the Broward County Sheriff's Office in Florida, Andy continues to educate others through his direct oversight of the training programs.

PACKTRACK

Acknowledgments

■ *(From left to right)* Instructors Romeo Ingreso, Brad Smith, Glen Anderson, Ron McCarthy, Jay Miller, and Pete Gallardo at the SKIDDS/CATS Class 162, Palm Springs, California.

Acknowledgments

WHILE I CANNOT THANK EVERYONE from whom I have received guidance over the years, I cannot overstate my appreciation to all the handlers, instructors, supervisors, and legal advisors who took the time to send pictures for and critique this book before it was published to ensure the information was correct. Many thanks to my co-authors, Jeff Barrett, Andy Weiman, and Ted Daus, whose contributions have made this book comprehensive and inclusive of all the K9 handling disciplines. I also thank all of my SKIDDS class instructors, who do an excellent job of spreading the word about K9s and SWAT working together. My sincere appreciation to the following people:

Adlerhorst Kennels
Attorney Jim Wilson, *ret.*
Attorney John Peters of John Peters PLC in Michigan
Attorney Taylor Rahn of Robles, Rael & Anaya, New Mexico
Attorney Tim Kral of Manning Kass & Ramirez, Los Angeles, CA
Designer Marisa Dirks of MDesign
Frank Rau of Pappy's Perspectives
John and Becky Johnston of AceK9.com
K9 Officer Dale Merchant and K9 Arlo, Garfield Heights (OH) PD, Master Trainer from the National Association of Professional Canine Handlers
K9 Officer Gordy Leitz, Mesa (AZ) Police Department
K9 Officer Ron Swart, Mesa (AZ) Police Department
K9 Officer Scott Callender, Mesa (AZ) Police Department
Laura Fogarty of Tactical Photography
Publisher and Editor Joanne Wolfe of Wolfe Media Resources
Rob Lukason, Asst. Chief USBP K9 Program Manager
Sgt. John Rolfe, Mesa (AZ) Police Department
Whitney Benoist of RoboteX

— *Brad Smith, Lake Havasu City*
December 2014

K9s In the Courtroom

Preface

LAWSUITS HAVE ALWAYS BEEN PART of police work, especially in cases where an officer uses force.

Back in the day, no one educated K9 handlers about civil litigation. We all knew lawsuits existed, but no one told us how to guard against them, or how to prepare for a lawsuit once it came. There were no K9 liability courses or seminars on how to write or update canine policy, select handlers and dogs, train and document that training, determine supervisor liability, make canine announcements prior to deployment, formulate tactics, write reports, or take bite pictures. Unlike today, there were no courses or seminars that explained what a set of interrogatories are, or how to prepare for a deposition or courtroom testimony.

We all essentially learned through on-the-job training (OJT) and prayed that no one named in the lawsuit would screw it up. Because I'm a guy who always believes the glass is half full, I would argue that, in many cases, civil litigation has been good for law enforcement. Time and again, we see how civil litigation has shaped agencies' training and recordkeeping for their K9 programs. Officers continually ask for more training from both in-house and outside training courses to learn how to do their jobs better and safer. Law enforcement should explore every avenue that can improve the quality of K9 units' training and performance.

However, in specialized assignments such as K9 and SWAT, training requests often are denied because of budget and personnel constraints. I realize that budgets are extremely tight, but why is training always the first thing to be cut? I find it incredibly humorous that nonexistant training funds suddenly become readily available after a department loses or settles a lawsuit. Training money miraculously

Preface

appears in the budget and, for a while, training becomes a priority.

When I began representing police departments in canine civil litigation as an expert witness, I realized that a lot of handlers and units were unprepared for what was about to happen to them. The sad thing is, no matter how prepared you are for a lawsuit, there's always the chance you will lose.

In today's high-tech world, we often see images and videos of officer-involved situations via the Internet. Millions of people are able to see, hear, and judge an officer's split-second decision making in situations that often are "tense, uncertain, and rapidly evolving." The Internet and social media provide nearly every U.S. citizen with a front-row seat to watch and re-watch every action and reaction of officers in the line of duty. That allows the public to draw uneducated conclusions and offer opinions about the world's finest law-enforcement personnel. Yet despite the rise of anti-police and anti-government feeling and the public's general distrust of our sworn testimony in court, we continue to find the educational tools to remain professionally elite and to meet society's ever-rising standards.

So how does one prepare for a lawsuit? There are some simple things you and your department can do to better prepare yourself for civil litigation, help reduce your liability, and increase your chances of winning in the court of public opinion. That is why I (Brad Smith) and the experts from HITS Training & Consulting are writing this book. In general, Brad Smith will cover liability for K9 patrol and K9 SWAT deployments, K9 Officer Jeff Barrett from HITS Training & Consulting will cover liability for tracking dogs, and Attorney Ted Daus and K9 Detective Andrew Weiman from HITS Training & Consulting will cover liability and successful courtroom presentations for detection dogs. However, several of us have added information to various sections throughout the book to bring you the most comprehensive perspective.

■ ■ ■

■ Your K9 has your back — make sure you have his by training smart and hard, keeping excellent records, and deploying wisely. If you do end up in court, the information in this book will help ensure that you can defend your actions and those of your K9 well.

Civil Litigation — Outrageous Payouts

■ Sooner or later, your K9 will bite someone, and you may very well end up in court.

MANY K9 HANDLERS, especially new handlers, will dismiss their chances of getting sued after their dog bites a suspect. We all have an abundance of self-confidence and believe that our efforts are soundly justified when using force and, more specifically, when our dog bites a suspect. I know this to be true from the many K9 cases I've been hired to help defend. Handlers who find themselves defendants in civil cases are stunned and taken aback by the realization that it did, in fact, happen to them. The resounding exclamations of utter surprise resonate through the halls of law-enforcement agencies everywhere.

In a simple public search of the Internet for settlements of civil litigation involving K9, I was able to find a small sampling. The staggering payouts listed in Table 1 are only the tip of the iceberg for out-of-court settlements and jury awards from lawful deployments and unintentional K9 injuries. Imagine the vast array of other civil litigations

K9s In the Courtroom

that bombard agencies on a daily basis. Agencies are constantly defending themselves against civil litigation for police brutality, destruction of property, false imprisonment, sexual harassment, and traffic accidents, to name a few types of cases.

Table 1. Civil litigation payouts

CALIFORNIA	NEW JERSEY	FLORIDA
$1.5 million	$150,000	$850,000
$500,000	$130,000	$153,000
$850,000	$115,000	$32,000
$240,000	$60,000	$7,500
$240,000	$30,000	
$225,000		TEXAS
$185,000	INDIANA	$77,500
$570,000	$85,000	
$79,500	$70,000	MARYLAND
$32,500		$125,000
	MINNESOTA	
WASHINGTON STATE	$65,000	OKLAHOMA
$1.5 million	$43,500	$15,000
$1,000,000		
$352,500	NEVADA	LOUSIANA
$350,000	$125,000	$14,000
$247,000	$11,000	
$230,000		PENNSYLVANIA
$175,000	NEW HAMPSHIRE	$300,000
$450,000	$85,000	$30,000
$412,000		
$225,000	NEBRASKA	ILLINOIS
$48,000	$43,800	$200,000
$25,000		
$17,000	IOWA	IDAHO
	$150,000	$61,000

■ ■ ■

Bulletproof Your K9 Unit

A "textbook" deployment?

A few years ago, I was hired by a department as their K9 expert in a K9 civil litigation lawsuit. During my meeting with the department's attorney, the K9 handler, his backup officers, and the K9 supervisor, we all agreed that the deployment was "textbook"; that is, everything was done as taught in basic training.

The suspect in this case was wanted for commercial burglary, grand theft auto, and assault with a deadly weapon. After a short pursuit, the suspect crashed the stolen car and fled on foot into a residential neighborhood. As they had been trained to do, the responding patrol officers resisted the natural urge to respond to the accident

■ Officers establish a perimeter and prepare to begin K9 announcements.

scene. Instead, the officers immediately established a perimeter, thus locking down the suspect, who was attempting to flee on foot.

During the next 45 minutes, as the perimeter was established and tactics were being discussed at the command post, numerous K9 announcements were made over the unit's PA system telling the suspect to give up peacefully or a police dog would be released and the suspect would be bitten. These K9 announcements were given from different positions around the perimeter. The K9 announcements also were recorded and time-stamped over the dispatch tapes.

Paramedics responded and staged next to the command post so they could provide immediate medical attention in the event the suspect or one of the officers was injured.

When the suspect refused to peacefully surrender, a K9 search was begun. Within 30 minutes, the dog alerted to the suspect hiding in the attic of a garage. More K9 announcements were given, and when the suspect refused to surrender peacefully, gas was inserted into the attic. When the suspect still did not surrender, the K9 was sent into the attic to locate him. The suspect was bitten on the leg and, after a short struggle, he surrendered. Paramedics responded, and within 2 minutes the suspect was being treated for his injuries.

The handler wrote a detailed report on the K9 deployment. The report included the three critical factors listed in *Graham v. Connor* to show the officer's use of force was reasonable. The three factors that were addressed, as stated by the United States Supreme Court, were: (1) the severity of the crime, (2) whether the suspect was a danger to officer(s) and the public, and (3) whether the suspect actively resisted arrest. During our meeting, the handler commented that he had read my book, *K9 Tactical Operations for Patrol and SWAT,* as well as my article in the Winter 2006 issue of *Police K-9 Magazine* titled "Report Writing 101 — Canine Use of Force," so he was well aware of what he needed to do in the deployment and what he needed to cover in his written report of the incident.

The suspect admitted, on tape, that he had committed all the crimes of which he was accused. He even admitted to hearing the K9 announce-

Chapter 2: Bulletproof Your K9 Unit

ments, but said he had not wanted to give up because he was on parole for weapons' possession and did not want to go back to prison. The perimeter officers also contacted neighbors and others who had heard the K9 announcements and witnessed portions of the incident so their observations could be documented and used to support the actions police had taken, in case a civil lawsuit should occur years later.

OK, I know what you're thinking at this point: "What's the lawsuit about?" This *does* sound like a textbook deployment, plus the suspect admitted to the crime, so why the lawsuit? How can someone file a lawsuit if that is what occurred?

The realities of civil litigation

Many years ago, a civil attorney answered those questions for me in the simplest of terms: anyone can file a civil lawsuit, and most of them will survive beyond the pleading stage and will continue in the litigation process, as long as the facts the plaintiff describes in the complaint "could have happened."

Many of these nuisance civil suits are dismissed without merit by the courts or won on motion of summary judgment (MSJ), but the process must take its course. It takes time and, of course, it costs the city or the county money — tax dollars — to defend their officers' actions.

The time and money that law-enforcement agencies must spend in dealing with false allegations profits the attorneys who represent the plaintiffs and keeps them coming back. Justice is not the only thing that a plaintiff or plaintiff's attorney are after; rather, they seek the financial benefit of an agreed-upon settlement or judgment to make them go away.

Unfortunately, some cities will give money to an attorney who has filed a nuisance lawsuit, simply to make him go away. Attorney networking is profitable, and it quickly becomes common knowledge which cities will pay up without much of a fight. Even if the police department did nothing wrong and plaintiff's attorney is willing to settle for $10,000 to $30,000, some cities will settle, because to fight and win the lawsuit will cost $50,000 to $100,000.

So in the short-sighted manner of housekeeping and watching out for our tax dollars, advocates would say that paying off a plaintiff is the right thing to do. Others however, would argue that fighting for what has been done correctly and legally will soon stop frivolous lawsuits, because attorneys will quickly realize there is little expectation of easy money coming from certain cities.

But I digress. As we looked over the lawsuit that the plaintiff's attorney filed, he made the standard claim of excessive use of force against the officers, but that was only the beginning. The suit also accused the officers of violating other Fourth and Fourteenth Amendment rights. To bolster their allegations, the plaintiff's attorney made false claims and used harsh and outrageous words and sentences to describe the K9 deployment as follows:
- "The officer intentionally used the police dog to attack my client under the color of authority."
- "Your actions were negligent and constituted improper conduct."
- "The arrest was unlawful and the force used to make the arrest was unnecessary, unreasonable, harmful, and offensive."

When a plaintiff's attorney finishes describing the incident, he or she will go to work on the dog and handler. Without even knowing the background of the dog and handler, they will try and strengthen their case by saying things such as:
- "The handler and police dog were improperly or inadequately trained and supervised."
- "The handler knew the dog was out of control and did nothing about it."

And last, but not least, without knowing the backgrounds of the department, the handler, or the supervisor, plaintiff's attorney will make outrageous claims such as:
- "The department failed to adequately discipline the K9 handlers and the officers involved for their actions of excessive force."
- "The department implemented, maintained, and tolerated policies, practices, and customs that contributed to your actions."

Chapter 2: Bulletproof Your K9 Unit

- "The department was negligent in its hiring of the officers."
- "The department did not properly train the officer."
- "The department did not properly supervise the officer."
- "The department was negligent in its retention of you before or after the incident."

Again, I know what some of you are thinking: those allegations have nothing to do with the K9 deployment; the deployment was textbook and the suspect admitted to the crime. Don't be naive enough to think that all the plaintiff's attorney is going to look at is the circumstances of the deployment. Plaintiff's attorney will try to stir up the waters as much as possible and see what floats to the surface.

By making outrageous claims, a plaintiff's attorney will get access to all your training records, your department manuals, your K9 manual, all your certification records, and whatever paperwork the courts will grant him access to.

The good, the bad, and the ugly

Now, back to the meeting. Although we all agreed this was a textbook deployment, as we began to look deeper into the department's inner workings, some major red flags went up. The areas of concern were:
- The department's lack of basic patrol K9 certification standards.
- The department's lack of annual recertification (there were none for the past seven years).
- The K9 policy.
- A lack of written training records and documentation.
- Lack of a K9 supervisor.
- Accidental bites.

The first red flag was the department's lack of basic patrol K9 certification and annual recertification. It turns out that this state was one of several that have no recommended training standard for patrol K9s. Rather than going to a reputable and recognized K9 organization and certifying to its patrol K9 standards, this department took it upon itself to come up with a departmental patrol K9 standard.

K9s In the Courtroom

That's fine, if the department's patrol K9 standard mirrors other recognized patrol K9 certifications and standards. In this case, however, both the standards and the personnel who did the certification were weak. The department's command staff, who had no K9 experience, were the ones who certified their department's patrol dogs before they went on the street.

The second red flag was the lack of annual K9 recertification. The K9 team had been on the street for nearly seven years and had never attempted nor completed an annual K9 recertification. Officers relied on their weekly K9 training to determine whether a dog was still streetworthy. Annual, independent, K9-team recertification is a measurement of continued maintenance. It is not the catch-all that saves all because it can be seen as a snapshot in time of the team's overall performance; rather, it is part of an agency's continuing efforts to show a level of competence in meeting a defined set of performance standards.

The third red flag was the department's K9 policy, which had not been updated in many years. I'm paraphrasing, but basically the K9 policy stated that if a person commits a crime (any crime), a dog could be used. Taking that literally, if someone stole a candy bar from a convenience store, a K9 could be used, and the handler would be within policy. Of course, the department's handlers knew better than to deploy in that type of situation, but you can see my point.

It would be easy to argue that the department lacked any real K9 policies to govern the K9 teams' deployments, and therefore did not regulate its use of the dogs. This lack essentially gave each of the handlers the authority to deploy without regard for the Fourth Amendment to the U.S. Constitution.

Luckily, there were a few green flags in this sea of red. *The first green flag* was that the K9 manual recommended that the K9 unit train 5 hours per week, or 20 hours per month. That is well above the industry standard of 4 hours per week or 16 hours per month. Officers also were encouraged to train on duty during slow times.

The second green flag was the unit's weekly K9 training sessions,

Chapter 2: Bulletproof Your K9 Unit

■ Training for tactical deployments helps ensure, and prove in court, that both K9 and handler are ready for the street.

which were not your standard, one-dimensional K9 training. Handlers did their basic K9 training, but they also worked on tactical deployments, so that the dog was exposed to many different tactical scenarios. The various levels of training, which included tactical scenario–based training, helped show that the K9 teams were ready for the street.

A third green flag was the outside training and schools the handlers attended. Although the department didn't always support their outside training requests, the handlers kept up-to-date on the latest training techniques and legal issues by attending courses in and around their region. Even if it meant they had to use vacation time and pay for their own travel expenses — such as hotel costs and class tuition — the handlers sacrificed out of their own pocket.

The fourth green flag was that handlers had a very good departmental in-service K9 training program. Handlers would conduct briefing training, during which they would discuss perimeter issues, K9 searching, movements, and tactical issues. The handlers even went so far as

K9s In the Courtroom

■ Attending outside training sessions and schools, even if it is on your own dime, shows the court that you have gone the extra mile in your training.

to demonstrate how to take the dog off a bite if they were to go down, and several officers had taken the dog off a bite in training.

The fifth green flag was that the K9 unit performed numerous public K9 demonstrations each year, and its officers spoke to many different businesses, organizations, civic groups, and schools to inform the public what their specialized unit was all about.

Now I know some of you don't like doing demos, but I am here to tell you that you are missing a wonderful opportunity to connect with, teach, and inform the public about what you do. Performing these necessary demos shows that your dog is friendly and under control. It's also a great way to interact with and enlighten any future jury members who may one day be sitting in a jury box deciding your fate.

But just when I thought the discussion was going well, *the fourth red flag* went up. I discovered that the unit's documentation of its weekly and advanced K9 training was not up-to-speed. The senior K9 handler sent an e-mail to the K9 sergeant each week, telling her what the K9 training was going to consist of or what classes they had taken, but that was it. No documentation existed on how the dog actually performed, and no certificate of completion was put into training or personnel files.

Chapter 2: Bulletproof Your K9 Unit

■ Handlers demonstrate high-quality in-service briefing training, in which they review and discuss perimeter and tactical issues, K9 searching, and movements.

Which brings me to *the fifth red flag:* K9 supervision. I discovered that the K9 sergeant and K9 lieutenant had no handler experience, which is common. Unfortunately, the K9 supervisors had not attended any classes to learn how to manage a K9 unit, and they had not been to K9 training in nearly a year. They basically supervised the K9 unit via e-mail, phone calls, memos, and reading the handlers' arrest and bite reports as those came across their desks. They felt that if they were not hearing about or seeing any problems, everything was OK.

The sixth and final red flag that came to light was the issue of accidental bites. Over the seven years this particular K9 team had been on the street, the dog had some accidental bites that resulted in nothing more than two letters of reprimand in his file.

To help reduce a city's liability, I know of some departments that have a policy of three strikes and you're out of the unit. Now before you get all excited, this department realized that sometimes there is nothing that can be done to prevent an accidental bite from occurring — such

K9s In the Courtroom

■ A K9 unit performs a public demonstration to help civilians understand what K9s do.

as an officer jumping out in front of the dog after the dog has been deployed. But hopefully that type of accidental bite will occur only once.

Decreasing liability due to accidental bites

When an accidental bite does occur, a department should look carefully at the details of each situation and provide remedial training and impose progressive discipline if the facts of the incident show the need for either or both.

The department should look not only at the dog, but at the handler as well. Too many departments get tunnel vision and think the dog is the problem. Supervisors should focus on the big picture and see whether there is a handler issue, or perhaps a bad dog and handler mix.

When an agency reviews the facts and circumstances of an accidental dog bite, the review should analyze the dog's general demeanor, the handler as a responsible party, and the team as it functions together. Far too often, an agency will be quick to assume that the dog is the sole trouble spot, when in reality, the dog may only be the sum of its environment and conditioning. Many times, failures are certain to happen because of a department's lack of understanding of the realm of law-enforcement K9 work.

Chapter 2: Bulletproof Your K9 Unit

When you look at accidental bites from a civil liability perspective, if a naïve administration fails to seek expert assistance in creating or maintaining its K9 unit, it should at least look to an expert's opinion when reviewing a series of accidental bites. A periodic external review can be helpful to an agency. Had this agency sought out an expert's review of their K9 unit's performance prior to having to use me, this agency probably would not have concluded that it should settle this particular lawsuit

The bottom line

In this case, even though the deployment was reasonable, lawful, and consistent with modern police K9 practices, standards, and departmental policies and procedures — as well as state statutes and case law — the department settled with the plaintiff before the case went to trial due to the problem of the many red flags raised by the unit's operating procedures.

For the next several years, while the plaintiff serves his time in prison, he has a large amount of money in his commissary account, compliments of this police department. This situation could have been avoided with proper education, training, and documentation

■ ■ ■

Chapter 3
Creating a Successful K9 Unit

AGENCIES THAT HAVE OR ARE THINKING ABOUT starting a K9 unit should step back and make an honest assessment about whether such a unit is truly needed. I realize that driving around in a K9 vehicle is cool, but unless there is both a real need and a careful selection of handler and K9, a department may be biting off more than it can chew, no pun intended.

As we consider the inherent potential for civil liability commonly associated with having a K9 unit, we must acknowledge and purposefully put into play the essential elements that create K9 success stories. As we discussed in Chapter 2, one of the key aspects of a K9 operation, which plaintiff's attorney will evaluate in deciding whether to file a lawsuit, is the unit's training program. Barring an absolute criminal act by the handler in using the dog, the facts and circumstances a civil attorney uses to construct a lawsuit are nearly always built upon a foundation of poor or insufficient training, documentation, or supervision.

The three basic areas that build a successful K9 unit are the right handler, the right dog, and the right training. To further strengthen those three essential elements, it is imperative to keep proper training and deployment records as a way to show that all three elements remain in good working order.

Good recordkeeping helps prove a K9 team's reliability. In other words, you're recording things that help prove to a jury that you were able to perform in the manner in which you say you deployed. Continuing education and additional training will be important ingredients and help support the idea that your K9 unit meets or exceeds current state or national standards.

Chapter 3: Creating a Successful K9 Unit

■ Keeping records of continuing education and additional training show the court that your K9 unit meets or exceeds state or national levels.

K9 performance on any level and in all disciplines is built on the theory that every K9 skill is perishable, and that performance levels will decline without frequent training. Hence the need for both training and evaluations to help prove reliability.

Creating a successful K9 unit isn't like purchasing a fleet of patrol cars or new pistols for everyone in the agency. You can't just read up on the latest trends and go with the lowest bids and expect the team to perform like every other team across the country. Prior to establishing a unit, your education should come from a reliable source, such as a well-established consultant whose advice is not influenced by third-party vendors. The consultant should be someone who will help guide the department in the right direction both for purchasing a dog and for training a team. The best way to beat a civil lawsuit is to do what you can to prevent one from ever being filed.

Selecting a vendor and trainer

Once you have decided to start a K9 unit — whether for patrol, detection, or just tracking — you'll then have to decide where to purchase dogs and who will provide training for the K9 teams. Don't assume that just anyone can supply your department with the quality dogs it needs. When it comes to selecting a K9 vendor, it's critical that you do your homework and research vendors carefully. Don't simply select the vendor closest to you, or the one that gives you the best deal or provides the lowest bid (does that reasoning sound familiar?).

Shortly after 9/11, numerous new K9 vendors emerged across the United States. Many offered unbelievable prices and said they could provide trained dogs within a few weeks. A number of departments purchased dogs without doing their due diligence. Within six to nine months, many of those new vendors had made a lot of money, but because they could not consistently deliver what they advertised, they had to close up shop and go elsewhere to offer their fraudulent claims, leaving their law-enforcement customers with less-than-optimal quality and poorly trained K9s.

Therefore, it's important to select a K9 vendor that is reputable, knowledgeable, and experienced in the law-enforcement K9 arena, and that guarantees its dogs. Be sure you ask about the owner's background, as well as the backgrounds of the instructors: they should have training or service in law enforcement. A civilian instructor can teach a police dog handler a lot, but there are many things — such as tactics — that a civilian instructor cannot teach. Also, instructors must be up-to-date on current K9 search techniques.

Whoever does your basic K9 training, make sure there is a very small student-to-instructor ratio. Many times I've seen basic K9 schools being taught with one instructor and 12 to 15 dog handlers. Unfortunately, there's not a lot of teaching or learning going on in such situations. The instructor is more of a manager than a trainer. A ratio of one instructor for every six to seven handlers would work out well.

Another reason it's important to have a small student/instructor ratio is to make sure the handler and dog are not simply being trained to pass certification tests, but rather to handle real-life situations and for that "what-if" moment. Be sure your trainer is challenging both the handler and the dog to prepare them for what they will face in the real world.

Chapter 3: Creating a Successful K9 Unit

This type of training can make all the difference on the street and in the courtroom.

Make sure your trainer provides written documentation of the training he or she will be giving your dog/handler team. The last thing you want to hear from your trainer is, "I'm not sure what we're going to do today; we'll just wing it." To keep the training going in the right direction, there should be a set course of instruction: a basic format and set of guidelines that can be customized as needed. The trainer also should be keeping written documentation of each day's activities and how the dogs preformed, even if just pass or fail.

If your trainer's background is strictly on the civilian–sport dog side, hopefully he has hired some current or prior law-enforcement handlers to assist in teaching the basic K9 course. The instructors should be knowledgeable about current case law and be able to answer any questions handlers may have. Even though your department's policy will provide K9 deployment guidelines, it's always helpful for handlers to be able to discuss basic K9 deployment issues during the course with an instructor who has been there and done that.

It's also important for the training staff to be up-to-date on current dog-training techniques rather than using analog training techniques and methods from the 1960s and '70s. The last thing you want to find out during a deposition is that the trainer has not updated or modified his training practices in 20 or 30 years.

Be cautious of basic K9 training courses that have a fast turnaround. In my opinion, unless you have an experienced handler being partnered with an experienced street dog, if a vendor or trainer says he can have a dog and handler trained and ready to work the street in two weeks, you should run the other way. Depending on the dog's experience and maturity, as well as what you are teaching the dog, a basic patrol K9 school may take as long as six to twelve weeks. An additional three to six weeks may be required to cross-train patrol dogs for detection work.

The last thing you should determine is your trainer's certification standards. Some states have specific training standards for patrol and detection dogs. If your state does not have such standards, make sure your vendor's certification training is up to the standards of a reputable national K9 organization such as the National Police Canine Association (NPCA), the North American Police Work Dog Association (NAPWDA), or the United States Police Canine Association (USPCA) — all of which have developed minimum training and certification standards for patrol and detection dogs. Sometimes the standards set by states or K9 organizations are minimal and basic. Preferably, your vendor is training and certifying to a higher standard.

I cannot overstate the importance of seeking a K9 expert's opinions and guidance in starting your unit. While I encourage you to do your homework and plenty of research on the vendors you might use, an independent K9 expert can be well worth extra peace of mind in knowing that you're not being taken advantage of by the vendor in both the quality of the dog and the training.

K9 policy

It is imperative that your agency have a written K9 policy before its unit is activated. Although that statement may appear silly on its face, there have been agencies that have fielded K9 teams while their policies and procedures were still being written. In so doing, those agencies needlessly exposed themselves to civil liability during the period that the policies and procedures remained a work in progress.

If you're not sure where to start, companies such as Lexipol sell formats and guidelines for creating K9 policy. Seek out an agency that has a K9 unit with a good reputation and ask for a copy of their policy. If it has a solid foundation, use it as a guide to draft your own.

Whatever means of guideline creation you select, make sure your K9 policy covers items such as:
- The K9 unit's purpose and scope
- The chain of command and responsibility within the K9 unit
- Dog and handler selection
- Daily, weekly, and monthly training requirements
- Off-duty responsibilities

Chapter 3: Creating a Successful K9 Unit

- Requirements for written documentation of training and deployments
- When a patrol K9 can be used
- K9 detection standards
- Guidelines for public demonstrations.

In general, K9 policies are much improved over what they were 25 years ago. From time to time you will see agencies whose K9 policies appear to have been written 30 or 40 years ago. Make sure your department's K9 policy is current and up-to-date. It would be wise to have an attorney who is well versed in using K9s for law enforcement review your K9 policy every two or three years.

Once the city or county attorney and the chief of police have approved the policy, the K9 unit's supervisor should document when each handler is given a copy of that policy. The dates that policy revisions are made should be on the bottom of every revision. This will show an active and ongoing review by the agency to stay current and up-to-date with current policing.

■ Once K9 policy has been approved, the K9 unit's supervisor should document when each handler receives a copy.

K9s In the Courtroom

Some agencies attempt to create a laundry list of when and where a police dog can be deployed. It is not advisable to have such a list, because it's impossible to think of every possible situation in which a police dog can or could be deployed. I prefer the simple approach to K9 deployment; that is, before a police service dog is released to search for a suspect, the handler and field supervisor should consider the following facts and determine whether the deployment is within policy. If these criteria are met, a police dog can be deployed during a patrol or SWAT operation. One must consider

- the severity of the crime
- whether the suspect poses a threat to the safety of law enforcement or others;
- whether the suspect is actively resisting or attempting to evade arrest; and
- what other means, if any, could be used to make the arrest.

Refer to Chapter 5 for more information on this subject.

Selecting a K9 handler

When it's time to select a new handler, a department must determine whether it has viable in-house candidates for the position. Many people think that the dog determines how good the K9 team will be, but in reality it is the handler who makes or breaks the success of the K9 team. We have a saying in the K9 world: "It goes right down the leash." Pair a mediocre dog with a good handler and that handler will make the dog better than anyone thought possible. However, pairing a good dog with a mediocre or poor handler will result in the dog having poor or mediocre street performances as well.

Another key to a smooth-running K9 team is to ensure that the dog and handler are a good fit. The last thing you want in a K9 team is a 90-mph dog paired with a 30-mph handler.

So what should you look for in a K9 handler? The ideal handler is an officer who is a hustler, a go-getter, and who is not afraid to work. A person to avoid is one who is happy being average. I don't know about you, but I don't want an average handler on my team. The ideal handler

Chapter 3: Creating a Successful K9 Unit

is one who is always trying to improve themselves and their dog. I believe it's important to review the officer's annual performance evaluations to determine what previous supervisors think of him. I also believe that it's important to review the officer's background to see whether they have sustained any use-of-force complaints.

Other important attributes of a desirable handler are a strong character, leadership ability, and good communication skills. It's also important that the handler has experience working in the field — patrol — because when a situation arises, officers at the command post will look to the handler to formulate a plan, communicate that plan to everyone, and then execute the plan. If you select a young, inexperienced officer, he or she likely will be overwhelmed in such a situation and the K9 team may be doomed to fail.

When it comes to actually selecting a new handler, in addition to the standard procedure of writing a memo and an oral board, some departments give potential handlers a physical fitness test to determine whether they are capable of performing the job on a daily basis and working with department K9s on obedience training and bite work. Be sure you don't lower the bar, and thus increase your agency's exposure to civil liability, by selecting a mediocre-to-average handler. I would rather leave a K9 handler position vacant than fill it with someone I know is not physically or mentally capable of top-notch performance.

The handler also needs to understand that his partner is not a pet, but rather a law-enforcement tool. If you take one thing from this book, it should be that we as K9 handlers must look at the bigger picture when it comes to our jobs. Think in more than one dimension by stepping out of your shoes and into the shoes of your bosses, other officers, and those who want to take money out of your pocket by suing you.

Remember, pets have very few rules and humans set expectations for their lives. As a result, they have very few responsibilities and fewer performance measures to achieve. A police dog's life is completely geared toward performance. The responsibilities that accompany and measure that performance rest squarely upon the shoulders of a K9 handler.

K9s In the Courtroom

Always remember that your police dog is your responsibility all the time. Structured, monitored, and controlled socialization should be a handler's goal.

Selecting a police dog

Back in the early days, handlers wanted the biggest, baddest, meanest dog around. They thought those characteristics would make a good patrol dog. Unfortunately, that couldn't be farther from the truth. In many cases, the handler got what he asked for but was unable to control the dog and make it do what was necessary to successfully work the street.

As I mentioned previously, you don't want that 90-mph dog paired with a 30-mph handler. It's extremely important to find a dog that both suits your law-enforcement needs and is compatible with the handler. Over the years I have learned that it's not necessarily the dog with the highest drive that makes the best patrol dog. Often, a medium-drive dog will work better on the street — do more and do it better than a higher-drive dog — because the handler will be better able to control the dog.

In my opinion, it's important to have a highly socialized dog. Some people think that a social dog won't engage on the street, but I'm here to tell you that is a false assumption. All three of the dogs I worked on the street over a 20-year period were extremely friendly: I could let them run around the police department and expose them to a lot of kids during school demos. Because of their sociability, I never worried about doing demos or neighborhood watch meetings. I'm always amazed when I run into dogs that have an extremely high defense drive and want to growl and bark at everyone who approaches them.

A strong, dominate dog, placed with a handler who is unable or unwilling to take control of the dog and manage the strong personality, will inevitably have accidental or unintended bites, resulting in lawsuits against the agency.

Make sure you select a dog you can control and that has the drives and courage you need, but one that also has the temperament to work well with trainers, handlers, and the general public. You never know when

Chapter 3: Creating a Successful K9 Unit

■ Because your K9 will often come into contact with noncriminal members of the public, it is important that your dog be well-socialized.

you might be asked to bring your dog into a courtroom so a jury can see it. The last thing you need is for the jury to hear your dog growling and barking at everyone in the hallway before you even enter the courtroom.

One of the biggest questions you must answer is whether you will buy a green dog versus a titled dog. A *green dog* is the term we use to describe a dog that has limited or no training. Such dogs typically are very young, but if they make it through law-enforcement training, they are likely to have a long career.

The term *titled dog* refers to one that is two or three years old and has earned a *Schutzhund* (protection dog) or *Koninklijke Nederlandse Politiehond Vereniging* (KNPV) title.

In addition to the training issue, another consideration in buying a titled dog versus a green dog is cost. Believe it or not, green dogs usually are only a few thousand dollars less than a titled dog. The one advantage to purchasing a titled dog is that the initial basic K9 training typically takes less time; sometimes as little as six weeks until the dog is ready to hit the street.

When considering a specific dog, you should test it before purchasing. I normally like to test the dog's obedience, walk the dog on slippery floors, see how it reacts to gunfire, determine whether the dog will go into a dark room, and evaluate its endurance and agility.

When testing several dogs, document each evaluation to ensure you select the best one for your department. I believe it's important for the K9 supervisor to be present during the selection process. Even if the supervisor relies on the trainer's recommendation to make the selection, in the chain of command, the K9 supervisor ultimately will have final approval.

Some agencies will test many dogs in one day. The testing can be video recorded for review at the end of the day. Some agencies also document each dog's review by using a preprinted work sheet that has a specific checklist. Such written documentation also can be reviewed to refresh your memory should more testing or evaluation need to be done prior to the final purchase.

Decoys

To the untrained eye, decoys are considered "bite dummies," and anyone can do the job. Nothing is farther from the truth. Decoys are an extremely important part of the dog's training — whether in a basic K9 course or in monthly maintenance training. When the dog is searching out of the handler's sight, the decoy is the one who gives the dog the proper corrections and modifies its behavior to conform to the handler's expectations, thus reaching the goal of the exercise.

Typically, a department's decoys are officers who are interested in becoming dog handlers, and who come to K9 training to learn as much as they can before they become part of the unit. For liability protection, a department should put an officer through decoy school before he or she is allowed to train with the K9 unit. Some departments have officers

Chapter 3: Creating a Successful K9 Unit

■ Decoys are an extremely important part of a dog's training and should be schooled accordingly.

sign a waiver prior to acting as a department decoy. Even if the decoy school is an "in-house" overview and introduction to the techniques and methods used by decoys, it should be documented as formal training for the volunteers who are attending.

K9 supervision

In some departments, the K9 supervisor is the weakest link. It would make sense to give charge of the unit to a sergeant or lieutenant who has handler experience — or at least someone who had the desire to be a handler prior to promotion. Unfortunately, some departments don't consider prior K9 experience a priority and assign a junior sergeant or junior lieutenant to oversee the unit. In many cases, the K9 supervisor never was a handler and had no desire to be one, doesn't like dogs, and doesn't particularly want to be a K9 supervisor. That is a recipe for disaster.

Such a K9 supervisor is unlikely to attend K9 training to see how the

K9s In the Courtroom

■ Instead of just attending training, supervisors should have periodic meetings with their handlers to see how they are doing and what they need.

unit is or is not performing. This K9 supervisor also is likely to deny most handler training requests because he does not see the need for more training, and when it comes to helping his handlers get new equipment, he may not go to bat for them with the department's administration.

Because that K9 supervisor lacks motivation, he will not want to attend a K9 supervisor school to learn what his duties are, as well as what he needs to do to protect the K9 unit from civil liability. Moreover, if a K9 handler is not self-motivated or becomes lazy to the point where his performance levels drop on the street and in training, the K9 supervisor will not be in a position to notice or care. The results of such inattentiveness and lack of supervision can easily be regarded by the court as negligent supervision and failure to properly supervise.

However, just because a supervisor has never been a handler does not automatically mean he will be a poor supervisor. In fact, some K9 supervisors who have never been handlers become outstanding K9 supervisors. They have embraced the supervisory opportunity and given it their all. They attend training at least twice a month, and they attend as many supervisor schools as they can so that they can learn to be the best supervisor possible.

Chapter 3: Creating a Successful K9 Unit

In addition to a K9 supervisor frequently attending the weekly training sessions, it is paramount that they review all of the written training documentation, deployment logs, and bite reports. In order to review K9 documentation, a K9 supervisor must understand terminology and jargon so that he or she can have a clear perception of what is occurring. Mere paper shuffling is meaningless, and inadequate supervision will be revealed quickly during a deposition with attorneys who will be looking for such weaknesses during a lawsuit.

■ ■ ■

Chapter 4
Training to Avoid Liability

Field training officer programs

I know it is not a common practice for most agencies, but I believe that instituting a two- to four-week K9 field training officer (FTO) program is an excellent way to reduce liability and prepare a new dog for the streets. Think back to when you graduated from the police academy. Were you ready to hit the streets on your first day at work, or did you need several weeks or months of additional training with an FTO before you felt comfortable being on your own? So why do departments — as soon as the dog graduates from basic K9 school — immediately put the dog and handler to work on the street without any additional training or handler guidance?

Unfortunately for some dogs, the best they will ever be trained is when they are fresh from basic K9 academy. A lot of handlers are placed on a beat and not allowed to train while on duty because calls for service have priority. Placing a new K9 team with a K9 FTO for a few weeks ensures a better-trained team that is more equipped to handle whatever dangerous situations arise on the street.

Dealing effectively with accidental bites

No matter how well we train, prepare, and protect law-enforcement officers and the public, accidental bites do occur. If such a situation arises, the handler should act professionally throughout the incident. The person who was bitten should be taken care of immediately and the handler should write a detailed report and make sure pictures are taken of the injured area.

Chapter 4: Training to Avoid Liability

Some agencies have a K9 liability settlement agreement in place for such occurrences. Although a department may want to go ahead and settle, in situations that are truly accidents the department would not be liable for the injury as a constitutional violation, because Section 1983 claims are based upon *intentional actions*. Furthermore, most states have created immunity for local governments and have not waived that immunity for mere negligence. Finally, even if the department is liable for negligence, the person who was bitten may have contributed to the injury.

When accidental bites occur, the K9 supervisor needs to evaluate the incident to see why it occurred. As we discussed in Chapter 2, many times departments think an accidental bite is a dog issue and do not look at the big picture. In some cases, it is a dog issue; but in a significant number of cases it is the handler who is the problem with the team. Again, this is a time to consider asking for a law-enforcement K9 expert's review — especially if accidental bites are happening frequently. It's important to determine what needs to be changed within the K9 policy, training, or deployments to correct the situation.

K9 settlement agreement

Your agency may already have a K9 settlement agreement in place for civilian accidental dog bites, but a K9 settlement agreement is not just for accidential K9 bites. In actuality, a settlement agreement and the accompanying process can be used in *any* accident that may occur during normal day-to-day operations. For example, an officer being the party at fault in a traffic accident or when a SWAT team is serving a search warrant and hits the wrong house, causing property damage.

However, since this book is about K9 liability, let's look at how a department can save thousands of dollars after an accidental dog bite. The first step is to have a plan in place before an accidental dog bite occurs. Contact your agency's legal counsel and discuss the creation of a K9 settlement agreement. Once your agency's legal counsel is on board with the idea and a procedure has been determined, most departments handle an accidental dog bite in the following manner:

- Immediate medical attention is provided to the person who was bitten.
- A supervisor — normally a sergeant or lieutenant — responds to the incident location.

   Some departments arrange for the agency's attorney or its risk manager to respond and handle the settlement process, rather than using a supervisor, to avoid later claims that the injured party was somehow intimidated into accepting the settlement offer made by an armed and uniformed peace officer.
- Audio- or videotape the entire process and negotiation.
- Once the person has been treated and released from the field or hospital, the supervisor or attorney will offer to pay all of the civilian's medical bills and negotiates an immediate monetary settlement.
- Some departments have a pre-set cash limit they can negotiate, while others will write a check for a specified amount.
- If a monetary settlement is reached, a Settlement Agreement form will be completed.
- Some attorneys may want the settlement agreement to include a prominent disclaimer that reads: "I acknowledge that I have had the opportunity to consult an attorney of my choice and have this agreement reviewed by such an attorney, but have elected to forego that opportunity and enter into this agreement as a final and binding settlement of any claims I may have against Officer _____ or the _____ Police Department."
- The civilian, the negotiator, and a witness all sign the document.
- Some agencies will want the Settlement Agreement notarized. If that is what your agency's attorney wants, be sure you have 24/7 access to a notary.
- Once the above process is finished and the person has received the money, the settlement is complete.

Maintenance training

Because of past civil litigation, a lot of departments have instituted a weekly K9 maintenance training program. The industry standard across

Chapter 4: Training to Avoid Liability

the United States is 4 hours per week or 16 hours per month. Those standards are echoed by national K9 organizations such as NPCA, NAPWDA, and USPCA.

The important thing to remember is that your K9 training should be documented and realistic. During your weekly or bi-monthly K9 team maintenance training, make sure you set aside time specifically for dog training. This is the time to improve your dog's capabilities or fix any issue your dog may have. Once your dog has learned the proper responses, it's time for tactical training. If you attempt tactical training first, before your dog understands what he is supposed to do, both you and your dog will become unnecessarily frustrated.

Unfortunately, many agencies do not have a full-time trainer, or even an experienced handler who has been designated as the department's K9 trainer. Often, K9 weekly maintenance training is unsupervised and has no set goals. It's highly recommend that K9 units formulate a *K9 training matrix* — a method used to track training and skill levels — to ensure that all members have a clear idea of what training will be performed and what the desired outcome will be. This format can always be modified if need be, but at least handlers will have an idea of what to expect during training.

During your K9 weekly maintenance training, you should debrief with the other handlers in your training group whatever real-world tactical situations happened in the week prior to training so that everyone can learn from them.

Not only should training be mentally challenging, it should be physically challenging as well. The K9 unit trainer must think and train outside the box. If all you do is basic K9 training, you and your dog will just be basic, or average — and hopefully no one wants to be average.

Advanced K9 training is critical

As I travel across the country teaching my SKIDDS and CATS classes, the overwhelming common shortfall is the lack of overall progression in the K9 team's abilities since they graduated from basic K9 school. My feeling is that handlers who remain average or at the basic, post-K9 academy level for both K9 control and tactics are more often than not setting themselves and their agency up for critical failures. Legal failures aside, the cost in human suffering resulting from a failure of this sort is unacceptable, and the resulting number of injuries to police officers is on the rise.

Many times, handlers incorrectly assume basic K9 training techniques as their tactical protocol. Handlers continue making grievous errors in their tactical deployments, based largely on what they learned in basic K9 school. Basic K9 schools are designed to build K9 control and teamwork through isolated training techniques that will be shaped and blended with more complex tasks in more stressful environments.

What fails to happen in many instances is trainers conditioning their young dogs to respond a certain way to the stimuli they might encounter at work, and therefore also conditioning the handlers in the same fashion. Failing to reshape and modify the handler's performance from the basic techniques used on the basic training grounds, to techniques that are proven more tactically sound, is a failure for us all.

■ Basic K9 school does not adequately prepare handlers for real-world tactical deployment; ongoing tactical training is critical to success.

Chapter 4: Training to Avoid Liability

Such gaps, if not filled in, will open a canyon large enough to allow civil litigation to freely drain the financial life from the agency, the K9 unit, and the individual officers themselves.

Following are some common examples of these types of basic failures:

- Immediately rushing in to help the dog in a fight with a suspect. If your first impulse is to rush the suspect once the dog is on the bite, your risk of being assaulted is tremendously high. Although that is commonly done during basic K9 school for several reasons, this technique should not be your standard method for apprehensions.
- Failure to use cover when it's readily available. Cover tactics are used more by rookie officers coming out of the police academy than by most seasoned K9 handlers. For some unexplainable reason, deploying the dog transforms K9 handlers into one-dimensional thinkers. We focus more on the dog's activities than on anything else around us. This phenomenon originates in basic K9 school, where we eagerly work to read and understand how K9s behave in searching and locating hidden suspects. Sadly, it can easily perpetuate itself as we continue our K9 careers. Often, we find ourselves leaving cover or ignoring cover for the sake of K9 control, K9 deployment direction efforts, and to maintain visual contact with the dog as it searches.
- The inability to verbally command a release from the bite during a real deployment. Many basic K9 schools work toward a certification objective. The K9 training techniques used in many K9 schools are heavily influenced by the need to achieve very specific goals for certification. In order to certify, the dogs are excessively exposed to the certification process, and the release from the bite under those conditions is instilled in the dog. Far less emphasis is placed on the release in other scenarios, and post–K9 school training regimens are less likely to advance the handler's abilities to achieve the release for fear that the dog will not engage or might have a poor grip. In either case, not having a verbal out from behind cover or from a distance can become a danger, both in the moment and in the courtroom.
- The inability to deploy on searches with cover officers. Handlers

frequently isolate themselves as an independent, self-sufficient, and self-reliant support unit for patrol. This ideology of independence, while common, isn't found in the majority of handlers to a debilitating degree, but it does seem to be frequent enough in the law-enforcement K9 realm for me to warn against it. Although ego and machismo are prevalent in our tactical units, handlers seldom benefit from acting as independent agents who prefer to work alone or who lack the ability to build a cohesive search team with their dogs. Little emphasis is placed on working the dog with multiple officers as cover during most basic K9 schools.

Recordkeeping

All the hard work you put into building your dog's performance means little in court if the documentation wasn't done or fails to adequately convey the dog's true abilities. Your word — even when you are sworn to tell the truth, the whole truth, and nothing but the truth — is not worth very much in front of today's juries and in the eyes of the courts. They hold law enforcement to a higher standard of proof, and part of that proof will be your records.

Two of the partners in HITS Training & Consulting, Jeff Barrett and Andy Weiman, have developed a recordkeeping software program called PACKTRACK, which is designed specifically to capture training issues and outcomes in written form. PACKTRACK helps handlers break down scenario-based training into its basic components so that each component is documented and readers can clearly see what has taken place. Often, handlers only write in their training records something like this:

"Today we did a tactical building search. There were two bad guys inside and we had to find them both. The dog did good, finding and biting both. One suspect tried to run and the other became aggressive."

PACKTRACK helps the handler to more specifically identify each component of the training scenario so that he or she gets credit for training in those areas. Without further details, the previous training description doesn't give the handler and dog much credit for what they

Chapter 4: Training to Avoid Liability

truly accomplished in that scenario. PACKTRACK identifies every element and asks the handler to comment on performance of each one.

For example, perhaps you didn't find it necessary to mention that in the scenario, the dog was required to jump over a barricade of tables set up by the decoy to stalemate the dog's pursuit (*agility performed*). Perhaps you did tactical obedience through the building as you sent the dog to search, commanded him into a "down," commanded him to return to the "heel," and directed him to "stay" while you moved to a better point of cover (*obedience performed*). During the capture, you might have commanded the dog to engage in the bite, disengage from the bite, or have physically removed him from it (*bite work with verbal and or physical outs*).

All of those elements are important aspects of training. They each hold relevance to your ability as a K9 team. PACKTRACK monitors how often you train those elements and can give you instant statistical data on each of them, so that you know how often or how seldom you've performed in those areas. Otherwise, such elements will have been wasted efforts in terms of a generalized summary of your training scenario. It's important that you thoroughly document your training to give you and your dog full credit for both skill level and practice of those skills.

Unit assessment

As I discussed in my previous book, *K9 Tactical Operations for Patrol and SWAT,* one of the things that's often lacking in departments is K9 assessment or audit. I repeat it here because its importance cannot be overstated. Audits are nothing new: professional sports teams and successful businesses periodically perform audits or evaluations that enable them to become better at what they do.

No one likes to think they need to improve, and some may think that an assessment suggests a weakness or problem in the K9 unit. Nothing could be farther from the truth. In fact, if you feel that way, I suggest that you may have an issue within your K9 unit that you don't want anyone to know about.

K9s In the Courtroom

Your K9 unit should go through two separate audits: an in-house evaluation and an outside evaluation performed by a qualified K9 expert. The in-house audit should occur at least once annually; the outside, independent audit should take place every three to five years.

Briefing and in-service training

When was the last time you trained with your patrol officers? In today's world, more cops are suing other cops than ever before. The primary reason for such lawsuits is that officers are saying they were never trained to work around a police dog. Therefore, I recommend that you provide briefing training to the officers you work with at a minimum of once every six months.

Training does not need to be long and elaborate, with PowerPoint slides, videos, and so on. Instead, simple briefings on topics such as perimeters, search formations, and arrest techniques can be accomplished in 3- to 5-minute training blocks.

Have you ever asked yourself or one of your patrol officers what they would do if your dog was biting a suspect, citizen, or patrol officer and you, the handler, were either injured or killed? Unless they have

■ Briefing training need not be long and elaborate; briefings on simple topics can be accomplished in 3- to 5-minute blocks.

Chapter 4: Training to Avoid Liability

been a dog handler, nearly 100 percent of the time their answer is that they would shoot the dog. When you think about it, that's not an outrageous answer, because they have no idea what else to do. It is our responsibility as handlers to teach the officers we work with what to do if you go down.

If you do training or instruct officers on any level departmentwide, down to the squad level, use a sign-in sheet to record who was there and the date. Write a brief overview of the training and how long it lasted. You have then created an essential piece of documentation that supports the training.

Ever since the mid-1980s, I have trained every police officer in my department what to do and how to properly take my dog off of a bite if I am unavailable. I'm not just talking theory; I actually have them do it. It's also one of the exercises I teach and have every student perform during my SWAT & K9s Interacting During Deployment School (SKIDDS) and CAnine Tactical School (CATS) courses.

Training for the street

One of my pet peeves is the handler who trains using only a hard sleeve. To me, that is unrealistic training that teaches the dog to focus on or target only one area of the body, as well as to look for equipment to bite.

Handlers should get away from training with a hard sleeve as soon as possible. One of the best ways to do that is through proper muzzle training, undercover work, using bite suits, and ground-fighting with the dog. When it comes to training for the street, hopefully the handler is recreating real-world deployments that have actually happened to him or to fellow officers.

As a trainer, you need to train your handlers to evaluate each situation to see whether it is truly a K9 operation. K9s are not always the answer to the problem. As an evaluator, have the handler verbally explain to you during training why they would or would not deploy the dog in a given situation.

Handlers oftentimes mentally overwork themselves as they attempt

K9s In the Courtroom

■ Stop training with a hard sleeve as soon as possible by using muzzle work, ground fighting, bite suits, and undercover work.

to apply the dog to every imaginable scenario that is presented to them. The dog is a tool and there are limitations to its capabilities. A good handler will explore the limitations in training and recognize commonsense scenarios that are outside those boundaries for a successful deployment.

As I mentioned previously, there is a time for dog behavioral training, and then there is a time for scenario-based training with backup officers. One of the issues I have seen in my classes is that when officers start to use cover and concealment and move in a tactical manner, some dogs become confused — they have not seen such behavior from the search team because the handler has not used it in K9 training. The dog then becomes more interested in the officers who are using cover and concealment (because it appears they are hiding) than in looking for the suspect.

Repeated exposure to scenarios that have higher degrees of stress for the team, especially the dog, will give the handler an opportunity to

Chapter 4: Training to Avoid Liability

■ Repeated exposure to high-stress training scenarios give the handler an opportunity to shape the dog's behavior and develop its performance.

shape the dog's behavior and develop its performance when it is deployed in the real world. During a lawsuit, K9 experts look for records that show these types of training setups, or the lack of them, as the case may be.

Overwhelming force

A lot of handlers think they can deploy their dog only during a tactical situation. Depending on the situation, however, there may be times when a handler is allowed to use what I call overwhelming force. *Overwhelming force,* if properly used, is not excessive force: it is essential, reasonable force that is combined with other less-lethal options to enhance the probability of a successful outcome. For example, there may be times when the dog is deployed at the same time that officers deploy a Taser, a bean bag, a distraction device, or a chemical agent. Refer to Chapter 5 for case law opinions on the use of force

■ Be sure to train your dog around all of the other less-lethal tools to avoid confusion in real-world scenarios.

during deployment.

The handler must make sure he or she has trained their dog around all of those less-lethal tools before the dog is put into a real-world situation with such tools. If you have not trained with items such as batons, Tasers, shields, bean bags, flash-bang devices, chemical agents, or with officers who are yelling at the suspect, you cannot know how your dog will react. You may be shocked to discover that your dog will not work or respond properly because it has not been exposed to such scenarios.

When it comes to training, make sure you are not simply training for certifications or competitions. There is a time for that, but you must ensure that your dog is street-worthy before you start worrying about police dog competitions.

Non-compliant or passive suspects

Handlers also should train their K9s in how to deal with passive suspects. Believe it or not, some dogs will not bite a passive suspect

Chapter 4: Training to Avoid Liability

because they have not been exposed to such a scenario. They are used to having the decoy stand in a corner or hide behind a door. When the dog is confronted with a passive suspect lying in the middle of a room, in a yard, or on a bed, the dog is confused and unsure what to do because the dog has never seen this picture before in training or real life.

Call-off and re-direct

Another thing handlers should train for while conducting a search is the call-off and re-direct. As a trainer, you can inform your handler that they will be looking for a decoy who is wearing some type of unique clothing — such as a blue bite suit. At some point during the search, the dog and handler will come across a decoy wearing a different color bite suit or clothing. Once the dog sees the decoy, the handler should be able to recall the dog and redirect it to another search area. Such situations are common in real-life deployments.

Don't be afraid to fail in training

Don't be afraid to make mistakes, or even to fail, in training. Make sure you push the envelope so that you can learn and be prepared for the real world. The time to make mistakes and learn from them is in training, not during a real deployment.

Understand that K9 experts are looking for documentation that shows where you had an unsuccessful training event or scenario. They also look for documentation on the methods you used to correct or overcome the issues where you or the dog were not successful. They look for training records that show relevance to job performance and how that training supported your assertions that the dog performed as it was supposed to or as you claim that it did.

Remember, your word alone isn't good enough; you must support it with well-documented training records that reflect a well-trained police K9 team.

■ ■ ■

Chapter 5

Avoiding K9 Deployment Errors

Foot pursuit or perimeter?
How you respond to this chapter will most likely depend on your age and experience. When I was a young officer, I wanted to chase everything that ran from me because "that's what cops do." That reaction has been imprinted onto our brains from all the TV shows we've watched over the years: Adam-12, T. J. Hooker, The Rookies, CHiPs, the original Hawaii Five-0, Hill Street Blues, and The Mod Squad (OK, now I'm *really* showing my age). For the younger generation, shows such as NCIS, Law & Order, COPS, Police Woman of Broward County, and Police Women of Maricopa County gave you that same message.

As we all know, foot pursuits are extremely dangerous. Deciding to initiate a foot pursuit is a decision that an officer must make quickly and under unpredictable and dynamic circumstances. The decision requires good judgment; sound tactics; heightened, simultaneous awareness of several factors; and good old-fashioned luck to avoid being injured or killed.

The majority of foot pursuits are initiated by individual officers who do not have immediate access to backup. Most foot pursuits are physically exhausting and, if a suspect is apprehended during a foot pursuit, a physical fight is likely to occur. Those factors increase the risk of serious injury or death for officers and suspects.

Danger for backup officers
When a foot pursuit is initiated, the one factor that is almost never thought of is the responding officers. They likely are driving to the scene

Chapter 5: Avoiding K9 Deployment Errors

at mach-1 speed, using their vehicle's emergency lights and siren, and they are placing themselves in danger while trying to get to your location. Sadly, how many times have we heard of or known officers who crashed their vehicles while driving to an officer-needing-assistance call and were injured — or worse, killed.

For the more seasoned and experienced officers who are reading this book, most of us have learned that making the conscious decision to set up a perimeter rather than going in foot pursuit will significantly reduce the chances that you *and* the backup officer will be injured or killed.

If you are the one responding as a backup officer, one of my pet peeves during a foot pursuit or when *any* officer requests emergency assistance is all the officers who get on the air just to say they are enroute. Don't you think everyone who is available is heading that way? Stay off the radio, keeping it clear so that the pursuing officer's broadcast isn't covered by someone saying they are enroute. If you *must* respond (if dispatch specifically requests a response), keep it as brief as possible: two words are really all that's necessary.

Making the wise move

Setting up a perimeter may not be as sexy or macho as engaging in a foot pursuit, but waiting for the cavalry to arrive before going after the suspect typically is the safest tactic for apprehending that suspect. Setting up a perimeter allows the use of superior force and firepower that results from adding additional personnel, proper tactical equipment, K9s, and air support.

However if you make the decision to pursue the suspect on foot, you should consider following at a distance while maintaining a visual on the suspect for as long as you can. As the pursuing officer, you need to clearly and calmly broadcast your call sign, location, direction of travel, the reason for the foot pursuit, the number of suspects and their description, and whether the suspect is known or believed to be armed.

Stop and evaluate

As the pursuing officer, once the suspect is out of sight you can use audible indicators such as dogs barking, fences rattling, gates closing, or the sound of a thud, which might indicate the suspect has fallen. Even quiet will let you know whether the suspect is still fleeing or has gone to ground. All those indicators will help you set up an effective perimeter.

If you can no longer see or hear the suspect, *stop* and set up a perimeter. There is no reason to blindly chase after someone you can no longer see. Stopping and evaluating the situation will significantly reduce your risk of being ambushed by the fleeing suspect, who may be armed and lying in wait to ambush the pursuing officer. Ceasing your pursuit and setting up a perimeter will reduce the possibility of being injured or killed.

Now I know what you are thinking: "I don't chase people, that's why I have a dog in the back of my car." True, releasing your dog from the back of your car could end the situation in a matter of seconds or minutes verses a matter of hours. However, before you release your dog, there are a number of things to consider. Here are a few of them:
- Are you alone, or is backup on-scene?
- What are the surroundings like?
- Is there more than one suspect?
- Time of day — is it rush hour in the city, nighttime, dusk or dawn, etc.?
- Are there citizen vehicles or pedestrian traffic in the area?

How many dogs are killed each year by handlers who release their dog to chase down a suspect, only to have the dog hit by a passing car as it chases the suspect across a roadway? Setting up a perimeter will reduce the chance of your K9 being injured or killed.

If you decide to send your dog after the fleeing suspect just remember, your dog will *lose suspect ID* for a brief moment as he exits the vehicle. Unless you have a group of highly trained and well-disciplined officers, I guarantee that someone is not going to wait for your dog to exit the vehicle. Officers will start chasing the suspect immediately and likely will pass your car before your dog has exited because "that's what cops do" and they want to be the hero.

Chapter 5: Avoiding K9 Deployment Errors

■ If you can no longer see or hear a suspect, stop and set up a perimeter.

I can see some of you shaking your head and smiling, so I think you see where I'm going with this. We have all heard stories of handlers releasing their dog just as an officer is running by their K9 unit or is already in front of them. We have all spent months, if not years, building our dogs' reputations only to see our efforts disappear in a matter of seconds when the dog bites the wrong person. Is it worth it?

An accidental bite means mounds of paperwork, memos, and weeks of apologies. With today's global media, there is a good chance your accidental bite will be on the 5 p.m., 6 p.m., and 10 p.m. news broadcasts for days, or on YouTube or Facebook before you even get to the hospital.

K9 deployment

As you know, I'm not an attorney, but I'm going to get a bit "lawyerly" and speak a little legalez in this chapter because it's vital that you hear, know, and understand what the courts have said about K9 deployments. Be sure you consult with your city attorney or legal representation if you have any questions.

During K9 civil litigation, plaintiff's attorney will alledge excessive force. Allegations of *excessive force* are examined under the Fourth Amendment's prohibition on *unreasonable seizures.* (See *Graham v. Connor,* 490 U.S. 386, 394 (1989) and (*Deorle v. Rutherford,* 272 F.3d 1272, 1279 (9th Cir. 2001)).

The *reasonableness* analysis in an excessive-force case is an objective one. Under *Graham v. Connor,* courts evaluate the government's interest in the use of force by examining three core factors: "the severity of the crime at issue, whether the suspect poses an immediate threat to the safety of the officers or others, and whether he is actively resisting arrest or attempting to evade arrest by flight." (*Graham,* 490 U.S. at 396; see also *Deorle,* 272 F.3d at 1280.)

However, recent case law has re-prioritized those three factors. Currently the most important factor under *Graham* is whether the suspect posed an "immediate threat to the safety of the officers or others." (*Smith v. City of Hemet,* 394 F.3d 689, 702 (9th Cir. 2005) (en banc) (quoting *Chew,* 27 F.3d at 1441).)

These factors, however, are not exclusive. Rather, courts should examine the totality of the circumstances and consider "whatever specific factors may be appropriate in a particular case, whether or not listed in *Graham.*" (*Franklin v. Foxworth,* 31 F.3d 873, 876 (9th Cir. 1994).) Such analysis allows the court to "determine objectively the amount of force that is necessary in a particular situation." (*Deorle,* 272 F.3d at 1280 (quoting *Graham,* 490 U.S. at 396-97).)

The analysis is limited to evaluating the objective facts and circumstances known to the officer at the time he used force to determine whether he had probable cause to believe that the person upon whom force was used posed a significant threat of death or physical injury to the officer or others. (*Graham v. Connor,* 490 U.S. 386, 397 (1989); *Doerle v. Rutherford,* 272 Fed.32d 1272, 1281; *Haugen v. Brosseau,* 351 F.3d 372, 387 (9th Cir. 2003); *Tennessee v. Garner,* 471 U.S. 1, 3 (1985).)

In lay terms, you will be judged on the information that was available to you at the time of the incident and the totality of the

Chapter 5: Avoiding K9 Deployment Errors

circumstances, rather than on 20/20 hindsight. Any facts that were learned after the officer used force may not be used later in evaluating whether the officer's decision to use force, or the level of force he chose to use, was "objectively reasonable."

"A simple statement by an officer that he fears for his safety or the safety of others is not enough. There must be objective factors to justify such a concern. A desire to quickly resolve a potentially dangerous situation is not the type of governmental interest that, standing alone, justifies the use of force that may cause serious injury." (*Deorle,* 272 F.3d at 1281.) Rather, the objective facts must indicate that the suspect poses an immediate threat to the officer or a member of the public.

Other force options

As I mentioned in Chapter 3, it is important to state in your report why lesser-force options were not used or would not have worked to take the suspect into custody safely. The 9th Circuit has also held that police are "required to consider what other tactics, if any, were available to effect the arrest." (*Headwaters,* 240 F.3d at 1204 (quoting *Chew,* 27 F.3d at 1443).

That court has stated, however, that this position is not intended to challenge the settled principle that police officers need not employ the "least intrusive" degree of force possible (see *Gregory v. County of Maui,* 523 F.3d 1103, 1107 (9th Cir. 2008) (citing *Forrester,* 25 F.3d at 807-08), but rather merely recognizes the equally settled principle that officers must consider less-intrusive methods of effecting the arrest, and that the presence of feasible alternatives is a factor to include in the reasonableness analysis. (*Bryan v. McPherson, supra.,* 590 F.3d 767.)

If you come to the conclusion that no other means of force is reasonable and prudent, that's fine as well. Just make sure you articulate those reasons clearly in your report.

Some of the reasons why other means of force are not practical could be as follows:
- Most of the time the suspect is hiding and you don't know where he is at.

- You have made numerous K9 announcements and the suspect has refused to peacefully surrender.
- Because you don't know where the suspect is hiding, the use of any other less-lethal means (command presence, control holds, batons, pepper spray, Tasers, beanbags, etc.) at that moment are either not working or are impractical.
- The distance of a visible suspect was too far way for a less-lethal tool to be used.
- The distance was too close for a less-lethal tool to be used.
- The use of a baton or control hold would mean the officers would have to leave their point of cover and approach the suspect to make direct contact, putting their lives in grave danger.

After considering all other less-lethal options at your disposal, you may decide that deploying the K9 is more practical and a much safer way to take the suspect into custody. That goes right along the lines of what the court has said in *Smith v. City of Hemet,* 394 F.3d 689, 702 (9th Cir. 2005): that one of the most important factors in using a dog is whether the suspect poses an immediate threat.

Control the rush

During every high-risk K9 tactical deployment, there's an adrenalin rush. If you don't feel that rush of excitement — and even fear the unknown — you're probably over-confident and not in the proper mindset to deploy. Most officers are able to handle such feelings because they have been trained to do so. It shouldn't be a debilitating fear or a nervousness that results in hesitation, confusion or a complete shut down, but rather a feeling of intense focus, determination, and mental clarity for the task at hand. Such adrenaline surges or rushes come from being well trained, well informed, and working as part of a cohesive team.

However, if you are about to do something you have never trained for — such as deploying your dog in a SWAT or high-risk patrol operation — don't. I realize it's hard to back away from a deployment, especially when you've been asked to be a part of a high-risk operation. But if you don't feel fully qualified, saying "no" is the right thing to do. If

Chapter 5: Avoiding K9 Deployment Errors

you deploy into a situation you've never trained for, you are asking for bad things to happen. Aside from the increased risk of loss of life, serious bodily injury, or a botched deployment, you're running the risk of creating more liability for yourself, the rest of the team, and the agency.

You'd be surprised at how many handlers show up to an incident and in less than five minutes are deploying their dog. But remember, stressful situations diminish your fine motor skills and make it more difficult to perform even simple tasks, such as leashing your dog. Don't overestimate the ability of your dog or yourself. If you do, you are asking for failure.

Know your limitations

Understand your dog's deployment capabilities and perhaps, even more importantly, you and your dog's limitations. Once you have a clear understanding of the operational plan and how you might be included in it, convey those things to the commanders in charge of the mission. They will be, or should be, looking to you for an informed opinion about using the dog in each operation. Be prepared to articulate the pros and cons from a K9 standpoint. Far too often, handlers overreach their trained potential in high-risk operations when looking for an angle to use the dog. The truth is, in a real-world incident, circumstances can arise that negate deployment of the dog with a SWAT team during the entry. Learn through training scenarios what is realistic for the dog to accomplish.

Who is in charge of the search team?

In most patrol K9 deployments, the on-scene supervisor will allow the handler to select the search team and control the search and tactics. Choose your search team wisely. Some of the larger law-enforcement agencies have a full-time SWAT team. So even on a high-risk patrol operation, the SWAT team can respond within a short time. For most of us, however, SWAT is a collateral duty, and there may only be a few — if any — SWAT operators working patrol at any given time. If you are fortunate enough to have some former or current SWAT members on duty, make sure they are on your search team, even if you have to bring them in from the perimeter.

I'm going to take this one step further. Even though this is a patrol operation and, as the handler, you are in charge of the tactics, in such situations I always relinquished the tactics to one of my officers who had SWAT experience and who understood how to work with the dog in a tactical situation. Doing so took a lot of the pressure off me and allowed me to do what I do best: to work and watch my dog. At times when I didn't have any SWAT operators on duty, I wore two hats: that of team leader and K9 handler.

Pre-deployment briefings and assignments

Once you have established that the K9 deployment meets the Fourth Amendment standards and is within departmental policy, there are a few things you might want to consider. Confirm that a perimeter is in place so that there are no weak areas where the suspect could escape.

Once you have selected your search team, hold a pre-deployment briefing. Some of the areas that should be covered in the briefing include:
- A synopsis of the crime and events leading up to the search
- Any statements that were made by the suspect(s)
- The suspect(s) description
- Whether the suspect(s) is armed
- Direction of suspect travel
- Whether K9 announcements have been given
- Review any officer down
- Review the location of the nearest human hospital and the nearest veterinarian trauma center.

During the briefing, assign officers their jobs on the search team. Someone should be assigned to the handler as a cover officer; other officers will be assigned to less-lethal, radio communication, and at least two officers to the arrest team. One of the arrest-team officers will assist you in hands-on control of the suspect; the second officer will provide lethal cover.

Chapter 5: Avoiding K9 Deployment Errors

■ When you have selected your search team, hold a pre-deployment briefing.

Be sure your search team knows the tactical plan, what you expect of them, and what their assignments are. Review the arrest techniques you plan to use if the suspect is found but a bite *has not* occurred, and what arrest techniques you will use if a bite has occurred.

During the search, do not drop your guard too soon. Don't assume there's only one suspect: always think, "Where there's one, there might be two." Be aware of any noise that could prematurely alert the suspect to your location. For example, we all carry cell phones. Double check that you have turned your cell phone to pleasure mode/vibrate so that your phone does not ring and give your position away.

During the search and arrest, avoid putting yourself — the handler — in a bad tactical position, such as out in front of the search team with no cover. Think officer safety and stay behind your team. Remember, your role in the search is K9 handler. Use your backup officers to clear the areas that your dog has already searched and indicated are safe to approach.

K9s In the Courtroom

Safety equipment

Handlers who deploy in patrol or SWAT need minimum safety and tactical equipment. Such equipment includes a Kevlar helmet, a tactical vest, and a gas mask. Even handlers assigned to a perimeter position or an arrest team need a gas mask in case chemical agents are deployed. Proper equipment will allow the handler to stay in place and not compromise the perimeter.

Make no mistake: every deployment — whether the suspect is thought or known to be armed — is a high-risk deployment, and every high-risk deployment requires proper safety equipment for all officers involved.

As a supervisor, do you want to be the one who has to explain in a deposition or in the courtroom why the handler was not properly equipped during a high-risk patrol or SWAT operation? Do you really think the excuse that there was "not enough money in the budget" or "we don't equip handlers with this type of basic safety equipment because they are not on SWAT," even though they are searching with SWAT, will be an adequate defense? I think not.

From the handler's perspective, if the department issues you this safety equipment, you'd better wear it. If you are injured and the safety equipment could have prevented the injury, how foolish and childish will it sound when you give the excuse that you did not wear the safety equipment because it was "too hot," "not comfortable," or "too heavy?"

■ Handlers who deploy with patrol or SWAT need, and should use, safety equipment.

Chapter 5: Avoiding K9 Deployment Errors

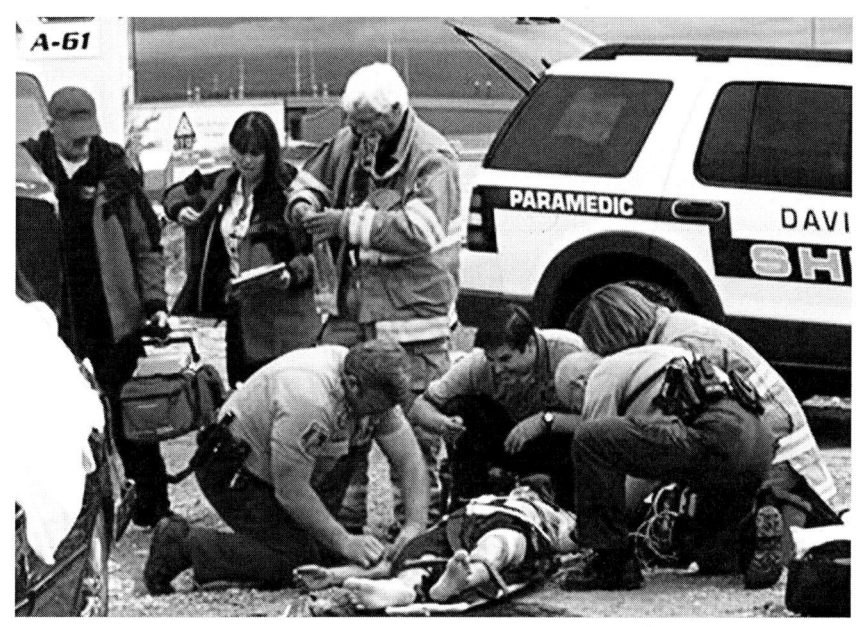

■ Make sure that you have medically trained officers or paramedics staged at the command post to quickly aid an injured suspect or officer.

Staging the heroes: paramedics on-scene

Today, one of the things civil attorneys sue police departments for is the lack of immediate medical attention provided for a suspect following an injury. If you do not have medically trained officers in your unit and your patrol division is not staging a paramedic unit at your command post when you have a perimeter established, I recommend that you consider staging such a unit as part of your standard procedures.

It can take paramedics as long as 10 minutes to arrive on-scene, so staging a paramedic unit at the command post allows quicker treatment of an injured suspect, *as well as immediate treatment of an injured officer* should that occur.

Some SWAT teams have the luxury of having a trained doctor or paramedic assigned to the team, but most patrol operations will rely on a staged paramedic at the command post. I recommend sending these doctors and all your fire paramedics to a basic veterinary K9 first-aid course and K9 trauma training in case the dog is injured as well. Most

K9s In the Courtroom

veterinarians will welcome the opportunity to train a tactical medic on K9 survival standards, and many will allow the medic to get hands-on experience by working in their office.

K9 bite pictures

In my work as an expert witness defending handlers who are involved in civil litigation, I see a lot of issues with K9 bite pictures. I frequently see bloody pictures someone took while paramedics were working on the suspect, or bloody pictures of the suspect lying in a hospital bed. Often, these pictures were taken from one or two feet away. Not only is that unnecessary, such pictures can come back to *bite you* in court. When I ask the officers why they took bloody pictures, I normally get one of two responses: they tell me that's what they've always done, or they say they did not take the pictures — another officer or CSI took them.

The bottom line is that it's unnecessary and unwise to take pictures while paramedics or doctors are working on the suspect. There will be

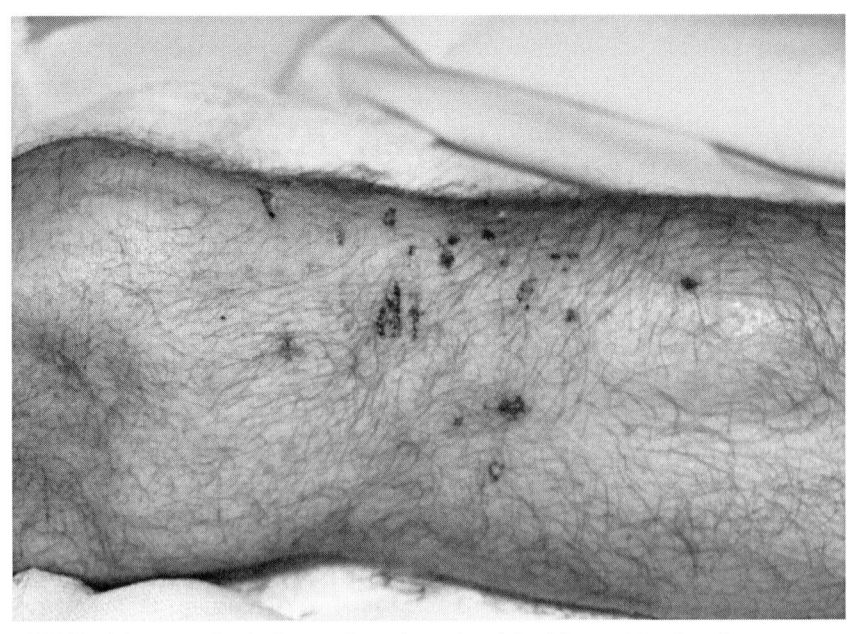

■ K9 bite pictures need only show a cleaned or sutured dog bite, post-treatment

Chapter 5: Avoiding K9 Deployment Errors

plenty of written documentation of the suspect's injuries and that the suspect received medical treatment. We are not in the business of dramatization; we are in the business of documenting the facts surrounding our actions. Pictures need only show a cleaned or sutured dog bite, which depicts the injury more accurately than showing a blood-covered arm from shoulder to wrist. Post-treatment pictures give the jury a true and factual representation of what happened, and your report can describe the existence of the injury and the medical aid rendered.

Therefore, before any pictures are taken, make sure all blood and debris have been cleared away from the injury. Be sure bloody towels and sheets are not in the picture and remember — Betadine on a white sheet looks like blood. Take your pictures against a clean and sterile background. Occasionally, you may not be able to get to the hospital to take clean pictures, so someone else will take them for you. Be sure you train other officers and CSIs to take only clean pictures.

Another potential problem is unofficial bite pictures taken from officers' personal or department-issued cell phones. *Don't take pictures at a crime scene unless you are using your cell phone to collect official evidence.* If you do use your cell phone to collect evidence, it's guaranteed your cell phone records will be subpoenaed to see whether you sent those pictures to anyone via text or email.

One thing that will help your defense in civil litigation is to take pictures of the suspect's entire body in the emergency room, so that his face and the rest of his body is photographed, including the injuries and tattoos. Such photos also will show where he is injured and where he is not. Such pictures will contrast with the suspect's cleaned-up appearance in court and will give the jury a more accurate look at the suspect as he or she appeared at the crime scene.

Some departments do not take pictures of suspect injuries. In one case I had, department representatives stated that it was not their department's policy to take pictures, and since the department did not supply the officers with cameras, they were not going to take pictures. I strongly recommend that if your department does not supply you with a camera, you purchase one and book the pictures into evidence.

■ Be sure to debrief following a search, whether or not the suspect was found or a bite occurred.

Debriefing the incident

After a search has been completed, it's important to debrief the entire incident, whether the suspect was found or a bite occurred. During the debriefing, you must honestly scrutinize and evaluate the deployment's successes and failures. Doing so is one of the best ways to achieve success in future tactical deployments. Don't be afraid to admit your mistakes so that you and others can learn from them.

During the post-deployment debriefing, you must be willing to examine what went right and what went wrong so that you can make corrections as needed. Future missions are more likely to fail if you have not recognized what caused breakdowns in prior deployments. Even small details that happened during the incident that did not follow protocol or didn't flow well with the tactical scheme you had envisioned should be discussed and analyzed to help guide future training goals and scenario-based training events.

■ ■ ■

Chapter 6

K9 Announcements

LIKE MOST OF US, I WAS TAUGHT IN BASIC K9 SCHOOL that I should always give a K9 announcement before I deployed my dog, unless articulable facts and officer safety concerns would made it dangerous to do so. However, one could argue that most, if not all, K9 deployments are high-risk and dangerous. Therefore, it's important to assess every incident carefully and decide whether a K9 announcement is appropriate. However, if you decide not to make a K9 announcement, be aware that you will have to justify your actions to a judge and jury, and if the only excuse you provide for not giving a K9 announcement is concern for officer safety, that might not be enough.

Where to give your K9 announcement

For the first year I worked my dog on the street, I always gave K9 announcements right before I released my dog. It made no difference whether those K9 announcements were given at the front door of a residence or commercial building, or whether I was about to deploy my dog into a backyard. I did as I was taught and gave the K9 announcements *from the entry point.*

I always felt "hung out to dry," because I was telling the suspect exactly where I was and that I was about to come looking for him by giving the K9 announcements right at the front door just moments before I made entry. I always felt there had to be a safer way to give K9 announcements but, like a lot of K9 handlers, I did what I was taught and did not adapt it to a real-life situations. One day on a SWAT callout, I realized there is a safer way to give K9 announcements. It was so

K9s In the Courtroom

■ Initial K9 announcements can be given from some distance away, using a public address system, thereby enhancing officer safety.

simple that I felt foolish for not thinking of it before.

Our SWAT team was serving an arrest warrant on a local gang member. I was initially placed on the perimeter with my dog in case the suspect ran. The SWAT team drove our Peacekeeper into the suspect's driveway and started making SWAT announcements for the gang member to peacefully come out of his residence and surrender to law enforcement. Several of his family members came out of the house, but he remained inside.

After everyone was out of the house, the officer who was giving the SWAT announcements then started making K9 announcements, which got me thinking, why didn't I use the same tactic in patrol? Why should

Chapter 6: K9 Announcements

I make my K9 announcement from the front door, when I could do it more safely by using the public address (PA) system in my patrol car?

The following night, while working patrol, we received a call of a burglary in progress at a residence. Patrol officers arrived quickly and set up a perimeter. When I arrived, I confirmed with the homeowner that no one should be inside the residence. I organized a search team and briefed them on the situation, as well as on how I planned to handle the K9 search. I advised the team that I was *not* going to give my K9 announcement at the open front door; instead, I was going to give it from my patrol car. I explained that if I gave my announcement at the front door, we'd have little cover or concealment. However, if the suspect did not surrender after I gave my K9 announcements at my patrol vehicle, we would quietly and tactically move up to the front door and deploy from there. Although this was something we had never done in patrol, you could see some of the officers understood that this was a better and safer way to do it.

After giving K9 announcements for approximately 10 minutes, the suspect eventually came out of the residence and surrendered. During our debriefing of the incident, the officers agreed that giving the announcements from the patrol vehicle enhanced our safety and allowed us a greater distance to deal with the suspect when he came out of the residence than we would have had if we had been stacked up at the front door.

Secondary K9 announcements

Using the PA system to give the initial announcements does not mean we don't give additional K9 announcements during the search. For example, if I'm inside a large building, at some point I will probably give a secondary announcement prior to releasing my dog farther into the location.

I always wait several minutes from the time I give my secondary K9 announcement until I release my dog. That gives the suspect ample opportunity to surrender, and it gives my dog and search team a brief rest.

K9s In the Courtroom

If the dog locates a suspect during the search, I recall my dog to my side and give the suspect one more opportunity to give up before opening the door and sending my dog into the room to find the suspect.

So remember, the tactics we are taught in basic K9 school are not always the safest tactics on the street. Often, we are taught a certain way in basic K9 school because that's how the certifications are written. I always say, train as you deploy. If you train unsafely, you will deploy unsafely. Sit down with members of your K9 unit or K9 officers from surrounding areas and discuss how you can deploy in a safer manner.

Mobile K9 announcements

Later that week, one of my detectives went in foot pursuit of a narcotics dealer and chased him through a residential neighborhood before losing sight of him. Patrol set up a quick perimeter and I was called in for a K9 search. When I arrived, I confirmed that a perimeter had been set up, and I talked with the detectives who were involved. As I do before every K9 search, I set up a search team, briefed them on the situation, and gave them their assignments.

I explained to my search team that I wanted to try a new tactic for my K9 announcements. I told them I thought it would be safer and more of a tactical advantage if I drove around our two-block perimeter and gave K9 announcements from my PA for approximately 5 minutes.

One of the detectives (a former SWAT operator) said, "Why? We've never done that before." I asked him whether he would rather we go up to the back gate, give my K9 announcement, and tell the suspect where we were at, or tactically move up to the rear gate and quietly release the dog into the backyard. It was like a light bulb appeared over the officers' heads.

For the next five minutes I drove around our two-block perimeter and gave numerous K9 announcements over my PA system. Several of the officers on perimeter stated over the radio that they could hear my K9 announcements loud and clear. As in the SWAT call-out, several citizens came out their homes to see what was going on. So I knew people inside their homes were hearing the K9 announcements and, if

Chapter 6: K9 Announcements

the suspect was in a backyard within the two block perimeter, he would hear the K9 announcements also.

After giving my K9 announcements, we waited for approximately five minutes to see whether the suspect would surrender peacefully. When the suspect did not surrender to any of the perimeter officers, we began our K9 search. After searching approximately eight houses, my dog found the suspect hiding in a backyard storage shed.

What the courts say about K9 announcements

The use of force by a police officer in the line of duty is determined under the Fourth Amendment's prohibition against unreasonable seizures (*Graham v. Connor,* 490 U.S. 386, 394 (1989)). Anytime your dog bites a suspect, it's considered a use of force under the Fourth Amendment.

As in the following cases, the courts generally require you give a canine announcement before deploying your dog.
- *Burrows v. City of Tulsa,* 25 F. 3d 1055 (1994) U.S. Court of Appeals Tenth Circuit
- *Trammell v. Thomason,* 335 Fed. Appx. 835 (2009)
- *Vathekan v. Prince George's County, MD,* 154 F. 3d 173 (Fourth Cir. 1998)
- *Kuha v. City of Minnetonka,* 365 F. 3d 590 (Eighth Cir. 2004)
- *Szabla v. City of Brooklyn Park, Minnesota,* 429 F. 3d 1168, 437 F. 3d 1289, 486 F. 3d 385 (U.S. Court of Appeals Eighth Circuit 2007)
- *Estate of Garcia v. City of Sacramento,* US Court of Appeals for Ninth circuit. 2014 U.S. App. LEXIS 3840 / 2014 WL 791813 — February 28, 2014

The most important factor under *Graham* is whether the suspect poses an "immediate threat to the safety of the officers or others." (*Smith v. City of Hemet,* 394 F.3d 689, 702 (9th Cir. 2005)). The facts and circumstances, which are legally relevant to the "objective reasonableness" determination, are only those that were known to the officer at the time the force was used. (*Graham,* 490 U.S. at p. 397)

As in the following cases, there are a few exceptions requiring K9

announcements for "officer safety reasons." But these three cases are the *exception,* not the rule. All of the three cases listed involved instances where the officer was facing an *imminent threat of death or great bodily harm,* and that is why a warning was not feasible:
- *Estate of Rodgers v. Smith,* 188 Fed. Appx. 175 (2006) 188 Fed. Appx. 175 (2006)
- *Thomson v. Salt Lake County,* 584 F. 3d 1304 (2009)
- *Crenshaw v. Lister,* 556 F. 3d 1283 (2009) 556 F. 3d 1283 (2009)

Another previously mentioned case you should be aware of in this instance is *Doerle v. Rutherford,* 272 Fed.32d 1272, 1281. *Doerle* is not a K9 case, it's a beanbag use-of-force case. In *Doerle,* the court held that law enforcement normally provides warnings in advance of using force where feasible, even when the force is less than deadly, and that the failure to give such a warning is a factor to consider in determining the reasonableness of the use of force. (See 272 F.3d at 1284). In this case, the officer did not give a verbal warning before using a beanbag and the officer was *not* granted qualified immunity by the courts.

And in *Jackson,* 268 F.3d at 653, the court said that the officer's safety interest increased further when the group *was warned* by police that a chemical irritant would be used if they did not move back, and the group refused to comply.

When a situation has slowed down and a perimeter has been established around a specific location or around a several block area, what's the hurry to deploy the dog? Have someone — either a handler or a patrol officer — give several K9 announcements while a plan is being formulated, a search team is being organized, and assignments are given out. Doing so will make the entire incident so much cleaner and easier to defend during a civil litigation.

What should your K9 announcements say?

It may sound strange because of all the emphasis that is put on K9 announcements, but the courts do not require that your warning be heard or understood. There is no way law enforcement can guarantee that 100 percent. What the courts say is that K9 announcements should

Chapter 6: K9 Announcements

be given in a way that *is likely to be* heard and understood.

To help you during a civil litigation, K9 announcements should contain certain information. The first part of your K9 announcement is that you are a law-enforcement officer from whatever department you are employed with. The second part of your K9 announcement should contain information about what you want the suspect to do. The third part of the K9 announcement should tell the suspect what will happen if he does not obey your announcement and surrender peacefully.

My K9 announcement sounded something like this: "This is the West Covina Police Department; surrender to the nearest police officer or *you will be bitten.*" Stop trying to be politically correct and get away from using the phrase *may be bitten.* There is nothing wrong with telling the suspect what will happen if they do not comply with your K9 announcements and surrender peacefully.

Another option in the announcement for a building search could be something like this, "This is the Lakeland Police Department's K9 unit. Make your presence known inside the building NOW by stating your name loudly before a police dog is sent in to find and bite you." Having any person inside the building verbalize their location in the search area rather than just appear without notice can be to your advantage. Initiating a dialogue with suspects or unforeseen innocent people inside can be less stressful and more manageable for the team than having someone popping out from around a corner and being right in your face.

Don't be in a hurry to deploy after your K9 announcements
Over the years, my department improved its method of giving K9 announcements. The the addition of a helicopter unit allows the department to give K9 announcements from the air as well as on the ground.

Another thing my department started to do was to key our radio mic during our K9 announcements. As we give our K9 announcements over the PA, someone keys their radio mic so that the K9 announcements are recorded through dispatch. Instead of our dispatchers telling us we have an open mic, we now have them trained to say over the radio,

K9s In the Courtroom

"Copy K9 announcements given at 2100 hours." During the following five minutes, we periodically key our mics so multiple K9 announcements are recorded. Our perimeter officers also have been taught to give their locations and respond over the radio when they hear the K9 announcements.

After giving your K9 announcements, *wait* for two or three minutes to see whether the suspect will surrender. If the suspect does not surrender, you can show the court and a jury that you tried everything you could to resolve this incident peacefully.

Just prior to starting our K9 search, we give the location of where the search will begin. Our dispatchers then respond, "Copy K9 search beginning at 2120 hours."

If the suspect is injured during the arrest, we make a copy of the dispatch tape and it is placed into evidence. Later, these recordings and time stamps can be very helpful in criminal and civil court as evidence that K9 announcements were actually given and what was said.

■ ■ ■

Chapter 7

Report Writing

What you need to know before you write your report

When law enforcement deploys a K9 to search for or apprehend a criminal, we know why we did it, but the *why* does not always make it into our incident reports clearly. An attorney I know has a couple of mottos: If an incident has occurred, ask yourself, "What went wrong and how can they blame it on me?" and "If something happened and it is not in your report, then it never happened." That goes for any use of force, not just K9 deployments.

So how can we use our reports to better defend our actions in court? First, handlers must always write extremely detailed reports. Second, we must know what the courts say about K9 depoyments and use of force and what the courts look for. If you have forgotten already, go back to Chapter 5 and review the listed case law. Third, think like a plaintiff's attorney. When plaintiff's attorney reads your report, think how they will try and make you look bad, and write a detailed report so that does not happen.

It's also important to document your efforts to bring each incident to a peaceful conclusion and to clearly articulate that if you had not taken the actions you did in deploying your K9, the incident could have had a more violent and dangerous outcome.

Justifying your use of force

Whether you use control holds, OC spray, a baton, a Taser, a beanbag, or a K9 to apprehend a suspect, you must write clear and articulate reports showing why your actions warranted the force used, as well as the length of time the force was used. When appropriate, explain why your actions did not create a substantial risk of causing death or serious bodily harm. It's also essential that officers report their state of mind during the incident, and what they intended the results of their use of force to be: to take the suspect into custody in the safest possible way.

As long as you are guided by the criteria established by the Fourth Amendment, by case law set forth in *Graham v. Connor* and the many cases since then articulating the law governing the use of force by peace officers, and can cite that guidance in your report, you can fully justify your actions in court. (Refer to Chapter 5 for more details.)

Although you cannot put every little detail into a report, putting in a little extra time when you write it will save you headaches later on. If you testify in court about a major aspect of an event that caused you to react as you did toward the suspect and it is not in your report, the plaintiff's attorney will ask, "If that event was so important, why didn't you put it into your report?" How will you then convince a jury that you are not making up the event?"

Of course, your report should include any announcements given before you deployed your K9, and whether you used a tape recorder or keyed your radio so that those announcements were recorded, as discussed in Chapter 6. You also should include a detailed account of what occurred when your dog found the suspect.

When I teach report writing for K9 handlers, my instuctions can seem abstract and broad in concept. Especially when each case will contain unique details and circumstances that will require the officer to be articulate in both content and explanation of how everything fits together, why decisions were made, and why results were justified. Failing to tie the details in your report to your thoughts at the time and how they affected your decisionmaking will fall short of the desired effect. Connect the dots for the jury so that they are able to connect with your reasoning during your deployment.

Have a clear understanding of the details and how each one helped guide your decisions to use force. Articulate the facts that were known to you before the deployment, the situational facts that developed dur-

Chapter 7: Report Writing

ing the deployment, and how each one of them helped you prepare for the deployment and adjust your use of force during the deployment by escalating it and then de-escalating it as the situation developed.

Post-deployment follow-up
After a K9 deployment, it's important to continue to gather information that will support the actions you took. I encourage you to delegate a team of officers — other than the handler — to talk with any citizens who may have observed the incident. The officers should get statements about what the bystanders saw and heard and should write a supplemental report to accompany the witness's statements, even if those witnesses say they saw and heard nothing. That ties bystanders to a story and provides a pathway to impeach a witness if they change their story later on.

I recommend that you audio record and then download and book these interviews as evidence. Witnesses will inevitably change and embellish their stories after they have talked to the suspect's attorneys or private investigators. Unfortunately, jurors no longer take an officer's word at face value and a mere supplemental report is not enough.

If no onlookers were observed on the street, knock on doors to get citizen statements. People may not have seen the incident, but they may have heard someone give a K9 announcement. If the suspect later says that he or she never heard the announcement, you can bring Joe and Jane Civilian into court to testify that the announcement was loudly given.

Take photographs of the immediate and surrounding areas where the suspect was found. Such photos can be used to show the tight and confined space the suspect was hiding in. If you see items such as hammers, screwdrivers, shovels, etc., in proximity to where the suspect was hiding and those items could be used to injure or kill you, take pictures of them as well.

I also took pictures of what the suspect could see from his point of view. Show whether the suspect had a clear view of the search team as you approached his hiding spot and how easy it would have been for

K9s In the Courtroom

him to ambush you as you searched for him

Document the time the suspect was taken into custody, when medical treatment was requested, when paramedics arrived, or how long it took you to transport the suspect to a hospital. Also, as previously noted in Chapter 5, take good clean pictures of the injury, if any, *after* it has been cleaned and sutured.

A complete and detailed report will ensure that you have good recall and written proof to back up your version of events in court.

Sample K9 bite report

The following sample bite report is reproduced here to help you understand the details that should be included in your own reports.

On 05/22/14, at approx. 0125 hours, K9 Rex and I responded to the 7-11 store located at 1626 W. San Bernardino Rd. to assist patrol units in searching for an attempted carjacking suspect, later identified as S-Jones.

When I arrived, officers informed me that S-Jones had attempted to carjack V-Patton at the nearby Arco Gas Station located at 1602 W. San Bernardino Rd. They told me that V-Patton said during the carjacking S-Jones stated he had a gun, but a gun was never seen. S-Jones had forcibly taken V-Patton's keys to the vehicle, got in the car, and attempted to drive away. When S-Jones could not get the car started, he was last seen running southbound through the alley to the rear of 1626 W. San Bernardino Rd. Refer to Officer Boyd's original report for details.

Officers Miller, Anderson, Critser, and Ramirez established a containment around the area. The perimeter consisted of Sunset to the east, San Bernardino to the north, Foxdale to the west, and Badillo to the south. I requested the assistance of LASD helicopter Air-45 to provide air support. I also requested a paramedic unit to stage at the command post, which was at the corner of Orange and San Bernardino Rd, to provide immediate medical attention if needed.

At 0145, while waiting for Air-45 to arrive, I drove my K9 unit around the perimeter and gave more than 15 K9 announcements over my unit's

Chapter 7: Report Writing

PA system for approx 10 minutes. The announcements advised S-Jones that we were the West Covina Police Department and he needed to come out of hiding and surrender to officers. They also advised S-Jones that if he did not surrender, a police dog would be used to search, and if he were found, he *would* be bitten.

As I drove around the perimeter in my K9 unit, officers keyed the mics on their hand-held radios so some of these announcements were recorded over the radio. The announcements were heard and acknowledged over the radio by the officers on the perimeter. S-Jones did not acknowledge my K9 announcement and did not peacefully surrender.

At 0200 hours, Air-45 arrived and made several orbits around the containment. They searched the area with their helicopter's searchlight and FLIR, but were unable to locate S-Jones.

At approx. 0210 hours, Air 45 also made several K9 announcements using the helicopter's PA system. The announcements advised S-Jones that the West Covina Police Department needed him to come out of hiding and surrender to officers. They also advised S-Jones that if he did not surrender, a police dog would be used to search and, if he were found, he *would* be bitten. I keyed my mic on my hand-held radio so some of the helicopter announcements were recorded over the radio. S-Jones still refused to surrender.

By 0220 hours, I had organized a K9 search team that consisted of Sergeant Benschop, Corporal Smith, Officer Serrano, Officer Barrett, and Officer Boyd.

At approx 0230, after conducting a pre-deployment briefing and giving S-Jones ample time of approx. 45 minutes to peacefully surrender, I took the criminal facts listed below into consideration for a K9 deployment:
• The suspect was wanted for 664/215(a) PC/attempted car jacking and 148(a)(1) PC, obstructing a police officer.
• The suspect had not been patted down, and stated he was armed with a gun.
• The suspect was familiar with the area he was hiding in and we were not.

K9s In the Courtroom

- The suspect was in an area with several hiding spots. The darkness of night and poor lighting conditions gave the suspect a strategic advantage over officers, and he could facilitate an ambush on the search team.
- As the suspect fled, he could have armed himself with common household items such as kitchen knives, hammers, a screwdriver, metal tools, large pieces of wood, or other items that could be used as weapons against the search team
- Over a 45-minute period, numerous K9 announcements were given over a helicopter's PA system, as well as my unit's PA, and were heard by officers on the perimeter, but the suspect refused to peacefully surrender.
- The suspect was actively resisting arrest by refusing to surrender despite several commands and announcements made by officers asking him to do so.
- The suspect's uncooperative and defiant behavior, and the fact the suspect may be armed with a gun, posed a danger to the officers and the community.
- Not attempting to arrest the suspect would put citizens living in the neighborhood in harm's way.
- Given his prior actions, there was a possibility that the suspect might attempt another carjacking, steal a vehicle to get away, or even break into someone's home and take a citizen hostage or do harm to the residence.

Based on the above facts, my intentions were to use K9 Rex as a locating tool and take S-Jones into custody in the safest manner possible for everyone involved. I also know that using police canines increases the likelihood that officers will apprehend suspects without the risk of having to use deadly force, especially when a suspect may be armed with a gun and is hiding inside a location. Using the police K9 in this manner can greatly enhance the safety of officers, bystanders, and suspects.

Lastly, the suspect controls what type, if any, use of force will be employed to take him into custody. If a suspect peacefully surrenders,

Chapter 7: Report Writing

no force is used. However, in this case, S-Jones would not give up after numerous K9 announcements. After careful thought and consideration, I decided to use K9 Rex to search for the suspect.

At approx. 0240 hours and after waiting nearly one hour for S-Jones to surrender, we started our K9 search down the alleyway to the rear of 1626 W. San Bernardino Rd.

I had Rex search ahead of the search team, off leash, to allow maximum distance and officer safety when the suspect was located. Within the first 50 feet, Rex showed interest near a large metal trashcan off to the right of the alley. After a few seconds, I could hear thumping sounds and could tell that Rex was engaged in a struggle.

The search team took cover behind several cars that were parked in the alley. I could not see S-Jones because he was concealed behind the large trashcan. All I could see was Rex's tail and Rex trying to pull S-Jones into the alley. I ordered S-Jones to show himself but he refused.

Corporal Smith and I moved forward to another vehicle so we could get a better view of S-Jones. At this point, I could see that Rex was biting S-Jones's right arm near his elbow and was trying to drag him toward us. I was ordering S-Jones to show his hands, surrender, and bring the dog to me. S-Jones still failed to comply with my commands and showed his defiance by hitting Rex on the head with his left fist and kicking Rex along the side of his body.

As the search team moved forward to take S-Jones into custody, I left Rex on the bite to distract S-Jones, keep him occupied, and keep him from running away. Corporal Smith, Officer Barrett, and Officer Serrano gained control of S-Jones and placed him in handcuffs. At this point, I had Rex release his bite of S-Jones, which he did immediately. Rex was on the bite for approx. 30 to 35 seconds. S-Jones was taken into custody at approx. 0244.

At approx. 0245, paramedics responded to our location, and in less then 2 minutes they were treating S-Jones. S-Jones was then transported to Queen of the Valley Hospital for medical attention, which was approx. 5 minutes away.

I took photographs of the scene and the area where S-Jones was found hiding behind a large trashcan. S-Jones had a clear and unobstructed view of the search team walking down the alley. No gun was found.

At the hospital, I noticed S-Jones had lacerations and puncture wounds on his right arm near his elbow. In addition, S-Jones had scratches and abrasions on both arms and wrists that appeared to be caused during the struggle.

While in the ER, I asked S-Jones if he had heard the K9 announcements being made. S-Jones said that he did not hear any of the announcements because he was asleep. S-Jones said he did not realize we were the police. He thought a stray dog was biting him. I also asked S-Jones if he would do anything differently if given the chance. S-Jones replied he would have come out quicker and just given up.

At the hospital, I spoke with Doctor Lee, who was treating S-Jones. I asked Doctor Lee about S-Jones's injuries and the doctor said none of them were life-threatening. I took photographs of S-Jones's injuries and booked them into evidence. I also had dispatch make a copy of the entire incident and place it on a CD. The CD also was placed into evidence.

■ ■ ■

Chapter 8

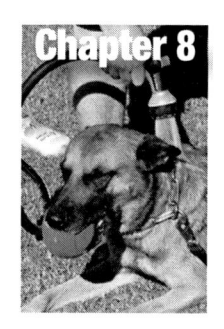

FLSA K9 Care and Maintenance

Fair Labor Standards Act

The Fair Labor Standards Act (FLSA) states that a person must be paid for all hours worked. That includes paying overtime if the person works more than 40 hours per week, even if the employer thinks the person could have finished the job in less time. FLSA especially applies to handlers who perform at-home care and maintenance for their K9 partners.

United States Department of Labor

The U.S. Department of Labor says that a handler must be compensated in some way for at-home care and maintenance of a police dog. If the time for at-home care and maintenance of a police dog means the handler is working more than 40 hours per week, the handler must be paid at time-and-a-half.

The main thing departments need to remember is that handler compensation for daily K9 care and maintenance is here to stay.

Numerous cases support handlers being compensated for K9 care and maintenance, but only one case gives a timeframe for that compensation: *Levering v. District of Columbia,* 869 F. Supp. 24 (1994). *Levering v. District of Columbia* states that a handler will spend 30 minutes per day, seven days a week, taking care of his dog. That equals a minimum of 3.5 hours per week in handler compensation. Those 3.5 hours can be paid at time-and-a-half compensation over your normal 40-hour work week, or it can be made a part of your normal 40-hour work week, which will mean a modified work schedule and less time on the street.

K9s In the Courtroom

■ The law says that handlers must be compensated for at-home care of a K9.

Case law
The following cases all uphold at-home K9 care and maintenance:
- *Truslow v. Spotsylvania County Sheriff*, 993 F. 2d 1539 (1993)
- *Nichols v. City of Chicago*, 789 F. Supp. 1438 (1992)
- *Levering v. District of Columbia*, 869 F. Supp. 24 (1994)
- *Reich v. New York City Transit Authority*, 45 F. 3d 646 (1995)
- *Andrews v. Dubois*, 888 F. Supp. 213 (1995)
- *Treece v. City of Little Rock, Arkansas*, 923 F. Supp. 1122 (1996)
- *Rudolph v. Metropolitan Airports Commission*, 103 F. 3d 677 (1996)
- *Mayhew v. Wells*, 125 F. 3d 216 (1997)
- *Albanese v. Bergen County, New Jersey*, 991 F. Supp. 410 (1998)

Chapter 8: FLSA K9 Care and Maintenance

- *Karr v. City of Beaumont, Texas*, 950 F. Supp. 1317 (1997)
- *Holzapfel v. Town of Newburgh, New York*, 145 F.3d 516 (1998)
- *Hellmers v. Town of Vestal, New York*, 969 F. Supp. 837 (1997)
- *Baker v. Stone County, Missouri*, 41 F. Supp. 2d 965 (1999)
- *Brock v. City of Cincinnati*, 236 F. 3d 793 (2001)
- *Howard v. City of Springfield, Illinois*, 274 F. 3d 1141 (2001)
- *Leever v. Carson City, Nevada*, 360 F. 3d 1014 (2004)
- *Letner v. City of Oliver Springs*, 545 F. Supp. 2d 717 (2008)
- *Scott v. City of New York*, 604 F. Supp. 2d 602 (2009)

Some of you may be saying, we have never asked our department for K9 care and maintenance, or our department still keeps denying us this right. If you have never asked your department for K9 care and maintenance, do so now. If you are told "no," or if the department has refused to pay you for K9 care and maintenance, hire a labor attorney, because it is highly likely you will win the case.

If you have never been compensated for K9 care and maintenance, you are allowed up to two years of back pay. It is easy to figure out how much you will receive in back pay. Take your hourly overtime rate x 3.5 hours per week x 104 weeks and that's your total. If your city has been fighting its K9 handlers on this issue, the courts can impose a punishment of one additional year — 52 weeks of additional back pay — to this formula. Likely the city also will have to pay the handlers' attorneys' fees. Some handlers work and care for two dogs. The department must compensate the handler for the extra time, equally, for each dog

As a side note, be aware that some agencies have waited until the courts finally forced them to pay handlers back pay for K9 care and maintenance, they did so reluctantly, then disbanded their K9 unit.

Chapter 9

Preparing for a Lawsuit

FOLLOWING ARE A FEW THINGS you should review to make sure you are prepared and up-to-date for any future litigation:
- Make sure your K9 policy is up-to-date.
- Your basic K9 training should be current.
- Monthly training should meet, and preferably exceed, the industry standard of 16 hours per month.
- You (the handler) should receive ongoing training away from the department.
- Re-certify your dog annually to state or national K9 association standards.
- Keep your training logs current; logs should reflect both good and bad results.
- Keep your FLSA K9 care and maintenance up-to-date.

What handlers can expect to be questioned about in court
- Did the deployment meet *Graham v. Connor* use-of-force standards?
- Were loud and clear K9 announcements given; if not, *why not?*
- Was the dog quiet during the announcements, or did the dog bark and cover up the sound of the announcements?
- Could the suspect hear the announcements?
- Did the handler maintain control of the dog?
- Did the suspect receive immediate medical attention, if needed?
- The bite report
- What training have you and the dog received?
- Department policy for other use-of-force tools

Chapter 9: Preparing for a Lawsuit

- Certifications and re-certifications
- Accidental bites, if any
- Citizen complaints
- Excessive-force complaints
- Why other, less-lethal tools were not used?

Get to know your attorney

One of the most important factors for a successful civil litigation is you. You can make a huge difference in your case. Your *attitude* towards the entire litigation process is something a lot of officers dismiss as irrelevant, but that could not be further from the truth. Your willingness to help in the defense of your own case is paramount. Your desire to work with and *educate* your attorney, as well as listen to your attorney's advice, is vital.

Any time you are notified that you are part of a civil litigation, it is imperative that you meet with your legal counsel as soon as possible. Remember, the attorney assigned to your case is *your* attorney, I know that sometimes frustrating things come up in lawsuits, but it's important to keep in mind that your attorney is on your side. Attorneys are not perfect, but they are there to help us.

You don't know what you don't know. Most officers will not know

■ Working with and educating your attorney about K9 is vital to winning your case.

what will be relevant to the lawsuit. On the flip side, the attorney will not necessarily know everything that is relevant in the law-enforcement context. Therefore, attorney and client must communicate about what they think is relevant to the case.

Meeting with your attorney will give you both the opportunity to ask any questions you may have and exchange personal contact information, including the best way to get in touch with each other without having to go through the department.

I'm sure that meeting with attorneys is not on your top 10 list of things to do, but I can't overemphasize the importance of this first meeting and any future meetings you will have. Besides your attorney getting to know you and your K9 background, it is *vital* that you learn how much your attorney knows about K9 cases. Just because your attorney is practicing law does not mean he or she is well-versed in K9 cases.

Hopefully your department has taken the time to hire an attorney who specializes in or has an extensive background in handling K9 cases. But don't be surprised if this is your attorney's first K9 case, and don't be surprised if you know more about K9 case law than your attorney does. Be prepared to spend extra time with your attorney getting him or her up to speed.

Trust your attorney: what you say to your attorney is confidential. If you try to hide something that you are embarrassed about or just do not want your attorney to know, it will eventually be discovered and it will hurt your case.

One of the best ways to educate your attorney is for the two of you to visit the location where the incident occurred. Also, I highly recommend that you invite your attorney to several of your weekly K9 trainings so they can see what you and your dog can do, as well as see how the dogs are trained. This will make your communication much easier when you are talking about the case and dogs in general. Your attorney will understand why you and your dog did what you did.

Once your attorney has attended some K9 training sessions and has learned about dogs and tactics, I would encourage you to invite your attorney to do some ride-alongs with you and your dog. The more

Chapter 9: Preparing for a Lawsuit

time you can spend together, the better defense team you will become.

Most attorneys will be grateful for any help you can give them, especially the attorney who knows little about K9 cases. If you find that your attorney is refusing to listen to you and your K9 advice, I would not hesitate to contact your risk manager or police association attorney and inform them of the K9 issues you are having with your attorney. You might even request that they look into getting an attorney who is experienced in K9 litigation, because it's your life and your future that is on the line.

Sometimes the pre-trial process will feel like "hurry up and wait." You may go for months without hearing anything from your attorneys, then they will be frantically trying to reach you. So feel free to call your attorney every once in a while to touch base. Your attorney has numerous other cases he is juggling along with yours, so he may forget that a certain deadline is approaching. Ask how the case is coming and when the next deadline will be? Your gentle reminder may be quite helpful.

Your attorney cannot control some aspects of the case. For example, the discovery process can be extremely invasive; so while your attorney should attempt to protect you from overly invasive questions or requests, just be aware that you may have to turn over documents or answer questions neither you nor your attorney want to. Also, litigation can take a long time: most of the delays will come from the plaintiff's side. You can "vent" to your attorney on how long the entire process is taking, but don't *take it out on* your attorney.

Interrogatories

The first time an officer may be aware that he or she is being sued is when, many years after the incident, someone hands them a set of discovery questions, known as *interrogatories*. These questions are what the plaintiff's attorney is asking you to recall about the incident.

Most departments have either the city attorney or a private law firm defend the city and the officer in the case. The attorney will pull all the reports, read them, and draft proposed responses to the interrogatory questions for you, based on the attorney's understanding of the facts gleaned from the reports, but you are the one signing or verifying these responses under penalty of perjury.

Some of the interrogatory questions will be objected to, but there will be some that must be answered. Therefore, when you are handed this set of interrogatory questions including proposed answers your attorney has already drafted for you, read them and make sure the answers are 100-percent accurate. If anything, however slight, needs to be changed, feel free to make those changes. Your attorney will not mind and, in fact, will appreciate your correcting the document. Once you sign the interrogatories on the last page, you will be married to those answers forever.

Before signing the last page, make sure you read not only your report, but also the reports of everyone who was on-scene. Carefully read through them and compare your report to the others. You may decide that you need to discuss the incident with the other people involved to refresh your memory, but proceed with caution, as any discussion with others outside the presence of your attorney is not privileged, and you may be creating witnesses who may inaccurately recall the topics of your discussion.

Request for production
There is another type of discovery known as *request for production,* which is simply requests for the city or the officer to turn over documents such as personal notes, cell phone records, and so on.

Depositions
The next step in the civil process is the deposition, which is more or less a fishing expedition. Cases can be won or lost at this stage of the process. Some officers will not even take the time to prepare for the deposition, they just wing it — an absolutely fatal error. That is the wrong attitude. You must prepare as though your life and livelihood depend on it, because in most cases, they do. You can *lose* a winnable civil case by not taking a few hours to prepare yourself and by giving a weak and feeble deposition.

Before your deposition date, be sure to meet with your attorney

Chapter 9: Preparing for a Lawsuit

— either one-on-one or, better yet, with others involved in the case — to discuss the case and hear what he expects from the plaintiff's attorney. There's nothing wrong, illegal, or unethical in meeting with your attorney before you testify in a deposition or courtroom trial, I guarantee the other side will do so. However, certain attorney–client privileges may be lost if the meeting includes people, such as a hired expert, not legally protected by the client-attorney relationship.

Know what the plaintiff is claiming in the lawsuit, as well as what the plaintiff's expert has written in his report about your deployment. When you read the claim for damages and the expert witness report, be prepared for the worst. His report will let you know what he intends to tell the jury about what he thinks you did wrong. The expert's main objective is to make you appear inept, unskilled, and untrained. Knowing the plaintiff's strategy allows you to counter his theories and build a strong defense.

Make sure you review all the incident reports, not just yours. As we discussed previously, during the deposition the plaintiff's attorney will ask you not only about the case, but also about your background, your department's use-of-force policy, and anything else he can think of, including the legal standards on when an officer may and may not use force.

When preparing for a deposition, don't imagine it's only about the case: prepare for the deposition as though it were a promotional exam. You need to articulate with grace and elegance all the policies relevant to your K9 deployment and use of force. Failure to clearly articulate to the jury that you know and understand your department's policies

■ Prepare for giving a deposition as well as you would prepare for a promotional exam.

K9s In the Courtroom

and procedures may change their opinion of you and of law enforcement. That could turn the tide against you and make them believe plaintiff's argument.

If you have given a deposition within the past five years, plaintiff's attorney may ask you questions about those incidents as well. Don't think he won't already know what cases you have testified or been deposed in previously. Plaintiff's attorneys have a network that keeps records of prior testimony by officers.

Plaintiff's attorney may try to trick you by asking a compound question and then requesting a "yes-or-no" answer. If you are confused about the question, don't hesitate to ask for clarification. Another way plaintiff's attorney may try to confuse you is to ask you a common question that sounds like a trick but is not. For example: "Is it possible for a dog to create serious bodily injury when he bites?" The obvious answer is, "Yes, it's possible." Don't be afraid to agree with plaintiff's attorney when its appropriate. Trying to dance around a question will only make you look evasive, as though you have something to hide.

If, at some point during the testimony, you realize that you misspoke, don't be afraid to speak up, admit your mistake, and correct it on record before it's too late.

Be prepared for your deposition to be videotaped: don't show up wearing shorts, a wife-beater T-shirt, and flip-flops. Dress professionally in either a Class A uniform, a clean K9 uniform, or a suit and tie. This may sound odd, but you might want to prepare yourself for being videotaped by setting up a video camera at home and simulating answering questions the attorney may ask you. That way, you will become more comfortable being videotaped, as well as see how you respond to the questions during the taping and whether you have any mannerisms that you wish to change. Such mannerisms could include starting sentences with "Uh," which can make you appear to be hesitant in your responses; shifting around in your seat a lot, which may make you appear to be nervous; or other mannerisms that make you look unprofessional.

If you are being videotaped, whenever possible, try to avoid overly long pauses before answering a question; such pauses may make you

Chapter 9: Preparing for a Lawsuit

seem evasive or uninformed. However, make sure you give your attorney time to object if need be. Think before you speak and don't look over at your attorney before answering a question. Avoid making unnecessary noises such as rustling papers, moving furniture, or touching the microphone. After a short time, you'll actually forget about the video camera.

Be aware that plaintiff's attorney is not your friend, and he will try to agitate you. You must be able to control your temper and not become argumentative. Also, be aware of body movements and nonverbal communication as you answer questions.

Plaintiff's attorneys will give you incomplete hypotheticals; vague, confusing and compound questions; misstate your report or prior testimony to see if you will agree with him; and will not follow the events' chronological order. All of that is intended to affect your testimony to his set of facts and be to his benefit.

One thing some officers are not aware of: as a named defendant in a civil lawsuit, you have the right to sit in and listen when other officers, witnesses, and even the plaintiff in your case, give their deposition testimonies. I strongly encourage you to take advantage of this valuable intelligence opportunity. It is likely you will be asked the same questions the other officers in the case are asked. Listening to them being questioned will give you the opportunity to prepare for what will be asked of you. But also be aware that the plaintiff has the right to be present at the officers' depositions. If this should happen, don't allow it to bother you.

The best general advice I can give you about giving a deposition is to tell the truth, act naturally, avoid slang or "police talk," and don't argue with counsel. A lot of the questions plaintiff's counsel will ask you can be answered with a "yes" or "no." Don't do plaintiff counsel's job for him by elaborating on the question or answering what you think he's asking. Make him work for the answer and ask the question more specifically in order to get the information he's looking for.

Don't jump the gun with your answers: make sure you listen to the entire question before you respond. Again, that will give your attorney the opportunity to object to the question if necessary. It also will give you a chance to think about the question and give the proper response.

A deposition may take two hours or eight hours. If you need to take a break at some point during the deposition, please don't hesitate to do so.

In a deposition, the rules are different than at trial. You may be asked questions that are insignificant, embarrassing, and appear to be unrelated to the incident. Your attorney may object, but in almost every case you will need to answer the question.

Depositions help plaintiff's counsel understand what kind of a witness you will be in front of a jury and how he wants to respond. By virtue of almost nonstop cross-examination during a deposition, a plaintiff's attorney will try to discover any weaknesses you may have. The attorney hopes you will say something that was not in the original report. Additionally, the attorney can, and often will, dig deeply into your personal background, formal education, police training, work history, and personal life, not to mention what you were doing days prior to the incident.

A lot of police officers think that because depositions are not held in a courtroom before a judge, they're not important. Nothing could be further from the truth. Plaintiff's attorney will try to make you feel comfortable by giving you complements about your training qualifications and so on, but don't be lulled into thinking he is on your side. In some instances, depositions can be more critical than the actual trial, because plaintiff's attorney will lock you into your version of the facts while you are under oath.

On the one hand, if you come across as a strong, knowledgeable, believable witness, plaintiff's attorney will get you off the stand as quickly as possible if the incident ever goes before a jury. On the other hand, if your weaknesses outweigh your strengths, you will be on the stand for a long time.

The courtroom

Most of you have testified in open court. However, if you've never testified in federal court, you need to know that although the process is similar, the atmosphere is very different. The first time I went to federal

Chapter 9: Preparing for a Lawsuit

■ Your role in the courtroom is to present your version of the facts in such a way that the jury will find your conduct reasonable, necessary, and proper.

court in downtown Los Angeles, I wore my uniform. As I went through the metal detectors, I quickly realized I would not be allowed to carry my handgun while walking through the courts. I had to secure my handgun in a locker. The feeling of walking around unarmed in full police uniform was highly uncomfortable. Later, I discovered that if I had worn a suit and tie, as a law-enforcement officer I would have been allowed to carry my handgun, because my jacket would have concealed it.

Remember, the courtroom is a theater for the trial lawyers. Your role is to present your version of the facts in such a way that the jury will see that your conduct was not only reasonable, but necessary and proper.

Trust me when I say that some jurors want to believe you as a law-enforcement officer. While the jury will hold you to a higher standard, they still want to believe you, as long as you can give them the confidence they're looking for from your side of the story. Plaintiff counsel's job is to try to stir up uncertainty, confusion, and generally muddy the waters as much as possible in order to create reasonable doubt.

K9s In the Courtroom

Unlike in criminal court where the verdict must be a unanimous 12–0, during a civil action in California state court the verdict does *not* have to be unanimous. A 9–3 vote will end the case. In a federal civil case, the jury must be unanimous, but there may only be six to eight jurors deciding the case.

As in the deposition process, make sure you listen to every question completely before you answer. On questions requiring a simple "yes" or "no," you can stay focused on the attorneys as you answer the questions. However, if a question requires a lengthy answer, make sure you turn and speak directly to the jury on occasion. Make eye contact with the jurors and answer the question in sufficient detail, avoiding police jargon, so that you are reasonably certain they understand your answer. Don't worry if some of your testimony is taken out of context. It is your attorney's job to clarify and set the record straight during redirect.

In a civil lawsuit, you must remember, this trial is about you. During a civil case you are the defendant, the *bad* guy. The criminal you arrested many years ago is considered the victim — the plaintiff in this case. In most criminal cases you participate in, you come to court, you testify, then you leave. For civil cases in which you are the defendant, you are required to sit at counsel's table during the trial, and the trial could take weeks or months.

It's not just about acting appropriately when you testify, but also when you are walking to and from the courthouse; in the parking lot; and inside the courtroom hallways, bathrooms, and cafeteria. During the course of the trial, from time to time you will run into members of the jury that holds your life and future in its collective hands. In most cases, jury members will see you more then you will see them. Act like the professional you are.

At some point in the trial, it would be helpful if your family, friends, and relatives could sit in the audience. The jurors will take note of this and realize that you are not simply a machine — you are human and have a family as well.

■ ■ ■

Chapter 10

Keeping a K9 Unit Running Smoothly

Still productive or burned out?
For 20 years of my 30-year law-enforcement career, I had the greatest job in the entire department: that of K9 handler. Whenever something went bad in the city or the surrounding areas, who did they call? Not Ghostbusters — the K9 unit.

As I travel around the country and people learn that I was a K9 handler for so many years, one of the things I'm frequently asked about is mandatory rotation. The inquiry normally comes from handlers who want to stay in the K9 unit but are close to their first dog's retirement.

Each department has its way of handling specialized assignments such as the K9 unit. Some departments allow the handler to stay in the unit as long as he or she is a productive member of the unit. That allows the handler to gain knowledge and experience so they can teach others what they have learned and make everyone's job safer.

Other departments have a mandatory rotation period, which does not allow a handler the opportunity to gain the experience and expertise that would help them become a trainer or an instructor and teach others what they have learned.

I understand the rationale behind mandatory rotation. It allows more department personnel to get experience, training, and background in various specialized units and become more "well-rounded" officers. But why do some administrators think they know what you want or what is best for your career to make you that well-rounded officer?

Many different types of people and personalities make up a police department and keep it running smoothly and efficiently. Some people like writing tickets, some like to take photos and fingerprints at crime scenes. Others like to work on computers and analyze crime statistics, and they do a great job. How many of those special assignments have mandatory rotations?

In most departments, once you are assigned to the detective bureau, you can stay there for the rest of your career. If you are assigned to the homicide desk, they don't make you work a different desk after a certain number of years or rotate you out of the bureau just to give others the opportunity to work homicide and become more well-rounded detectives. The department wants to keep you in place because of the training and expertise you have developed.

Departments must keep in mind that some people have little desire for promotion because they like what they do and are extremely good at their job. For some, it may seem that the natural progression of an officer's career is to move up the promotional ladder. But for others, there is another progressive career path that is more appealing: the progressive, upward climb toward becoming highly specialized in a given law-enforcement unit — an expert in one specific area.

Many administrators fail to see the true value of investing in and cultivating a select group of men and women who eagerly look forward to becoming highly trained professionals. Rotation for the sake of career development of the individual is far from being a positive idea. It is a theoretical masterpiece that falls woefully short of any real or meaningful effect for the person, the department, or the community. Often, mandatory rotations reduce individual morale and thus the overall department morale. They also deplete depth of knowledge for the entire unit and increase the potential for litigation — especially in the K9 unit.

Not everyone wants to stay in K9 for as long as I did — or as long as the other handlers who have co-authored this book — but thankfully, none of us were subjected to mandatory rotations. The short list of those who choose to stay in the K9 unit and continue learning and honing their K9 skills often becomes a silent and valuable resource for their agencies.

Mature, well-trained, experienced K9 handlers repeatedly make

Chapter 10: Keeping a K9 Unit Running Smoothly

better decisions in how and when they deploy. Their level of training and K9 control is higher, they have better written reports, and their training records are well-worded and articulate. They've learned to be verbally articulate when giving court testimony — what to say and what not to say. All of those things help save lives, produce more arrests, and can remarkably reduce civil litigation.

Stay or leave?

As with anything else, there are pros and cons to both sides of the mandatory rotation argument. If you want to continue to be a handler, don't give your department any option but to leave you in the K9 unit. Show your supervisors you are a leader and that you hold yourself to a higher standard. By your actions, you can raise the bar for other handlers who come into the K9 unit.

Don't just be the K9 handler who "waits for the big call." Go out every day and be proactive in your duties as a police officer. Make sure you continued to grow and develop your expertise as a dog handler, and share your knowledge and skills with others in the unit as well as in surrounding departments. Being proactive might mean that you attend classes on your own time and your own dime, but it will be worth it in the end.

However, if you are a supervisor who has a handler who has grown stagnant, has a bad attitude, or is always calling in sick, I would agree that you should get that handler out of the unit. You know the type — the person who has been a handler for X amount of years but is still a one-year handler. Some officers look for a unit to hide out in, where they're not inundated with call after call for police service. Some see the K9 unit as that place to hide. What those officers fail to see is the amount of work is takes to be a good K9 handler. Good management can weed out the deadwood. Rotation out for poor performance is essential for individual growth, department morale, and productivity.

Also, if your department has a small, one- or two-person K9 unit, I might understand the reasoning behind wanting a built-in rotation. But again, look at the handler and see what kind of job they are doing. If you are always rotating new personnel into the K9 unit, you will not have anyone with real-world expertise to bring other new handlers along and help them with any issues that occur. And trust me, if you are working with dogs, problems will occur.

If you decide to have mandatory rotation in the K9 unit, you might want to consider having one position that is permanent. But that permanent position is only for the handler that has shown the greatest leadership, commitment, and dedication to the K9 unit and truly deserves the position.

Remember, the K9 unit probably has the greatest potential for civil litigation within the department. Look around your department: you know the officers who want to be handlers. Do you really want some of those people in the unit? With mandatory rotation, you may get what you asked for — rotation — but that may result in bigger problems.

Pressures handlers face

You always risk the possibility of burnout by allowing a handler to stay in the K9 unit too long. As a K9 unit supervisor, you must be aware of some of the signs and symptoms of K9 burnout and know how to deal with it, should it occur in your unit.

A handler may get burned out for any of several reasons. When officers are first selected to be handlers, they are normally excited and committed to the job at hand. Unfortunately for some, devotion and enthusiasm do not last forever. The handler may be under a lot of pressure at home because they are always away training, working, or getting called out.

Some handlers feel pressure from their peers because they are always under the microscope and expected to always find the suspect. Some handlers bring the pressure on themselves; they may have trouble saying "no" and are overwhelmed by other collateral duties they are performing within the department or in their personal lives.

Even harder for the seasoned handler is knowing when to say enough is enough and it's time for me to move on. Some handlers feel that if they leave the K9 unit, especially before their dog is ready to

Chapter 10: Keeping a K9 Unit Running Smoothly

retire, they are quitters. As a K9 supervisor, it may become necessary for you to do the hard yet correct thing and remove them from the K9 unit.

How to recognize K9 burnout

There may be several indicators that a handler is getting burned out. As a K9 supervisor, you should be attending the weekly K9 trainings so that you can make sure your unit is maintaining its high standards. One of the first clues someone may be burned out is that their dog's performance starts to decline because the handler starts to make excuses why he can't attend the weekly maintenance training.

If you are not able to attend all of the K9 trainings, keep an eye on your unit's training and deployment records. Make sure each handler is attending your weekly maintenance training and that each of your handlers is doing all of the exercises that were scheduled for that day.

Another clue may be that the handler acts as though he is no longer able to dedicate the necessary time and energy to making the proper preparations for a successful training session. And once the training is underway, the handler does not want to participate.

Every officer has the right to use his or her vacation or comp time. Because of that benefit, there will be times when a handler will not be able to attend weekly K9 training due to a scheduled vacations. But an increase in the amount of absenteeism from scheduled training could be a red flag. If you see your handler missing a lot of scheduled training or his training logs show he is not maintaining the recommended 16 hours per month maintenance training, you need to find out why.

Another red flag of possible burnout is the handler's reliability when it comes to being available and responding to calls for service, as well as to callouts from home. Where once you were able to rely on this person to pick up the phone on the first ring or call you back within 30 seconds of leaving a message, now the handler is never available for callouts and never returns your calls

K9 demonstrations and public speaking are part of a K9 handler's duties. You used to be able to rely on the handler wearing a clean uniform, having a clean dog, and showing off an exceptionally clean K9 unit whenever he did a public event. Now the handler arrives with a dirty uniform, filthy K9 unit, and a smelly dog.

A benefit most supervisors don't think about when they go to K9 training is to observe and listen to what handlers have to say about each other. All specialized units joke, haze, and tease each other, but it is done in a fun way and meant to give you constructive criticism and ways to improve. But as a supervisor, if you listen to the comments of handlers in your unit, as well as those from other units that attend your weekly K9 training, you will soon be able to tell the difference between joking and teasing with constructive criticisms versus truly negative comments.

You will hear and feel if the other handlers express frustration and lack of commitment toward one of their fellow officers because of his lack of training, performance, and professionalism. The other handlers' body language also will give you a hint that they are frustrated with this handler and his lack of commitment, dedication, and enthusiasm.

Supervisor responsibility

For most K9 supervisors, the hardest aspect of approaching a burned-out handler is that the handler probably is one of the senior members of the K9 unit and, at one point during his career, he might have been held in high regard within the department for his experience, expertise, and skills as a handler. He also may have been instrumental in the unit's success. There's also the chance the K9 supervisor and handler are good friends, and probably have been in battle together. The history between the two of you is something only law-enforcement can understand and comprehend. But allowing your emotions to override your duty as a supervisor ultimately is doing a disservice to the handler, the K9 unit, and the department.

Once you recognize the signs of possible burnout, you must take immediate action. Call the handler aside, away from the other handlers and all distractions, and be as upfront and candid as possible about the situation. Let him know exactly what has led you to this moment by telling him what you've seen, read, and heard and ask him why

Chapter 10: Keeping a K9 Unit Running Smoothly

these things are occurring.

You may find there is a valid reason why the handler has been acting the way he has. There may be a personal or deep family issue or illness that no one in the department knows about because the handler is a very private person and does not want to burden anyone at work. And, let's face it, some of us are just too proud and stubborn to ask anyone for help.

You may discover that your actions have forced the handler to confide in someone about the utter turmoil and chaos that is going on in his life right now. Doing so might help relieve some of the internal pressure he has been holding onto and he may be willing to seek professional help. In some cases, all the handler needed was for someone to care enough to ask what is going on and listen to him.

Then again, you may find that there is no personal or family issue underlying how the handler has been performing. If that is the case, make it clear that the handler's performance is unacceptable. Let him know that you see signs of burnout, and ask him whether there's anything you can do to help him improve his performance.

Make sure the handler understands that the burden of change is on him. If his training and job performance do not improve within a specified timeframe, there will be severe consequences, which may result in him being removed from the K9 unit.

Like anything else in today's world, you should not only document this meeting, but also articulate the timeline for improvement and implement a weekly performance evaluation to document the handler's improvements or lack thereof. The handler should sign each weekly evaluation form and be given a copy.

You also may discover that the handler has been looking for a way out of the unit for a long time, but did not have the courage and fortitude to ask for help or leave the unit on his own.

We all like to be recognized for our accomplishments. If the handler decides the best thing would be for him to leave the unit, make sure the handler leaves with honor, dignity, and a sense of achievement in what he has done over the years. It may be as simple as giving him a plaque commemorating his years of service on his last K9 training day, or the handler receiving a unit citation or recognition during briefing or in front of the City Council.

After the handler has been out of the unit for a while and has recharged his batteries, you might want to ask him if he would be willing to come back and assist the K9 unit from time to time by sharing his experience and expertise with new handlers that come into the unit.

You don't have to be a supervisor to recognize burnout. If any handler, trainer, or instructor recognizes some of the signs and symptoms of burnout discussed in this chapter, bring them to your supervisor's attention so the issue can be dealt with immediately. It might save your fellow officer's career.

■ ■ ■

K9 Tracking — This Book Should Change Your K9 Life

Proving your worth
The infamous declaration that a police dog is, first and foremost, a locating tool, means that you must not only prove your *own* worth by finding what you set out to find, you also must legitimize your *dog's* capabilities. Throughout this book, each of the authors repeatedly highlights the necessity for K9 recordkeeping. The point of recordkeeping is not simply to produce a binder full of regimented and repetitive documents showing that you were alive, somewhat coherent, and doing well during your department's scheduled training days, but rather to create vivid images of a forward-moving and progressive path of successes that show a well-trained and reliable police dog. Because of the popularity of using patrol dogs to track, there's a good chance that people will be bitten. Your training and recordkeeping will come into question frequently in both the criminal prosecution and the civil litigation processes.

There is little dispute that police dogs that have been trained to hunt humans by trailing odors and require frequent and recurring training to maintain an adequate degree of success. Much like other K9 disciplines, tracking is a perishable skill and therefore is always subject to the scrutiny of the courts. As a result, final analysis of a K9 team's performance will rest on the quality of the training logs produced. Not only does the K9 handler have to consider what to write in his or her training logs, the handler also must understand the training techniques used to accomplish the goal of shaping a dog's abilities to track.

Watching a guilty criminal being freed because you couldn't prove your dog's reliability has a significant impact on many fronts; to have that same criminal file a civil suit against you and your agency is a personal punch to the gut that should shock our society's moral conscience. Sadly, such lawsuits have become so commonplace that society supports the idea as a civil mechanism for balancing what is seen as heavy-handed government. Having been involved in a number of civil lawsuits over the course of 32 years in the criminal justice system and as an expert K9 witness, I've received quite an educational gift from those who seek monetary compensation. Those lessons learned allow me to "pay it forward" and help educate K9 handlers. Trailing with reckless abandon behind a tracking dog is as careless as ignoring the advice given in this book. Who wants to walk into a courtroom in which the judge says, "Will the defendant please rise?" as he looks straight at you? The tactics discussed in this chapter are as real and as important to your K9 life as any other situational awareness in your career.

K9 terminology

The semantics inherent in K9 terminology spans each discipline, and I want to cut straight to the chase here. Dogs that are trained to find criminals who have fled on foot use their olfactory systems, take in odors, process them in the brain, and make decisions about following those odors; in those ways they are no different from any dog. What makes them different is that police K9s perform based on the conditioning they've received through training, and they routinely produce remarkable and successful results. However, you need to know that using terms such as *tracking, trailing, wind scenting,* and the like in court will be used against you. Pick any term and the experts will argue against it, as they try to toss a red herring into the courtroom to convince listeners that your training methods are not reliable, or that what you did in the actual deployment is not consistent with your training. It's going to happen. But one thing is certain: no human has been able to replicate the conditions under which you and your dog performed during a real-world deployment. Prosecutors will interpret your written and spoken word and form an opinion about how inefficient you were in training and

Chapter 11: K9 Tracking —This Book Should Change Your K9 Life

during the deployment. So when you use various terms, be aware that they may have subtle variances, but the main objective is steadfast: to have the K9 acquire certain odors and follow them to a successful end, semantics notwithstanding.

Every K9 trainer and K9 expert will draw lines in the sand with terminology. Don't sweat it! It's not the terminology that matters, it's the techniques used in training and all the variations of the training that count toward proving K9 reliability.

Does the beginning define the end?

You'll hear much talk within the law-enforcement K9 community about how a dog has been trained to track, with emphasis on getting started, transitions, and broadening the dog's capabilities. As I travel across the country and enjoy opportunities to discuss tracking with hundreds of police K9 handlers, I often get asked about techniques for teaching a dog to track. Typically, my answer is as follows. Every dog is somewhat different in its genetic makeup and level of drive to perform, and many proven techniques exist that produce effective results. Find techniques that marry well with your dog's makeup and proceed. Read books on training dogs to track, attend seminars that give you hands-on tracking training, and talk with successful people to learn what they've done to accomplish a higher level of K9 tracking. When experts attempt to tear down your dog's reliability, generally they'll attack your foundation training first. To define their claims of inadequate performance, they will make assertions such as

• The dog was insufficiently trained to track by an independent source, outside of law enforcement, prior to the handler receiving the dog. No records support the assertion of skill level.

• The training techniques used for this dog began with a foundation based on sport dog philosophies, which do not lend themselves to police work and therefore provide no credibility in establishing reliability in this case.

• The foundational training techniques used to train this dog to track were predicated exclusively on the dog's survival instinct. Food was the

K9s In the Courtroom

motivating force for the dog to track, resulting in an inherent desire for the dog to feed along the track. Combine that with the genetic drive to capture prey and the dog has been purposefully reverted to an instinctual predator: therefore, the dog is more likely to attack someone without provocation.
• The initial tracking training appears to have been flawed by lack of proper technique. Over-stimulation and overuse of aggression has produced a dog that is not capable of following tracks that are more than 2 minutes old or are not pre-stimulated by aggression and the headlong flight of the quarry.

As you can see from those four examples, the first attack is on the foundation. Even proven dogs that have tracked for six or more years can be called into question by such misguiding analytics. If you were completely ignorant about police work and police dog training, you could easily be led up a garden path without roses. Yet, in my opinion, what's been documented in training for the six months prior to the deployment at issue is far more relevant than what occurred during the *first* six months of the dog's initial training. Although all K9 training records can lend themselves to supporting specific elements of an event, what has taken place in your K9 training during the recent past can be of more value to the individuals whose opinions will be shaped by what we can prove, and who will ultimately judge us. The beginning of training is simply that: the beginning. Progression and transitions that are clearly documented in your training records will eliminate false ideas that will surely be presented as truth and fact in defining K9 reliability.

Your K9 records show that you encourage bad behavior

Along our K9 career path, we pick up many catch phrases along with our helpful training techniques. For the most part, these unique terms are short and to the point; they're frequently benign and exemplify exactly what took place. As an example, one of the most popular sayings in patrol dog training is, "The dog was given a reward bite." Many of us don't see this phrase as anything other than a way to quickly define a valid training technique for patrol dogs. We all know that

Chapter 11: K9 Tracking — This Book Should Change Your K9 Life

pursuit of the bite is one of the most ambitious drives a patrol dog can possess and develop.

Manipulating the dog's performances with such a reward system is commonplace. However, laypeople may gasp in disbelief and conjure up images of rogue cops unleashing their hounds upon defenseless citizens as a means of rewarding and furthering the most hellish of behaviors ever displayed by mankind in a state ruled by out-of-control cops. Trust me, that's a view shared by many, glamorized by Hollywood, and perpetuated by the claims of those who find themselves on the wrong side of the law. So what's the real deal here and what are we doing wrong?

There's nothing wrong with the training techniques; however, clarification of the terminology can go a long way in diverting the cries of foul play, abuse, and the like when the plaintiff's experts pick over your records. My position is that rewarding the dog with a bite for finding the helper's hidden location not only gives the handler the opportunity to provide satisfaction to the dog for a job well done, it also moves the team into a stage of bite-work training. Perhaps you're building a better grip, building K9 confidence in a struggle, or evaluating the dog's commitment to staying solidly engaged for an extended time. Perhaps you need to address release of the bite under various conditions and for various reasons. Perhaps you think that the "real training" was only about the search or the track and the bite was merely a reward. I encourage you to consider all aspects of the training exercise as quality time and to record all of them in detail.

To address the reward bite more directly, aside from moving into bite-work training, we must consider protective equipment as nothing more than an oversized toy. If we intended to have the dog bite as a reward, the equipment is there solely to prevent serious injury to the helper who is wearing it. A standard toy can be used, but the helper is not protected from an accidental bite — after all, we are dealing with dogs that are trained to bite and that display high levels of aggression. Moreover, for many dogs the simulation of apprehending prey is more satisfying than the traditional tennis ball reward.

K9s In the Courtroom

If the bite is part of a scenario-based training exercise, it might not be given for the purpose of a reward; often, muzzles are used in lieu of bite equipment, even for some tracking training. Make a clear distinction in your records about what constitutes a mere reward bite from a bite that is prompted for other reasons. Having a clear understanding of the difference will help you document for the reader what training took place and why.

The spontaneous bite at the end of your tracks

Officer-safety concerns won't keep you from writing checks payable to the suspect. Many K9 handlers and trainers advocate conditioning their dogs to spontaneously bite at the end of a track when the suspect has been located, provided the dog is able to get to the suspect. The motivating factors in that training philosophy are numerous, but officer safety is frequently touted as the primary reason. Although at first glance that type of training seems safest, the dynamics of each real-world deployment present K9 handlers with much more complex decision-making than simply biting a suspect spontaneously once he is found. A bitten suspect is rarely an incapacitated suspect, and the fever-pitch atmosphere that ensues upon engagement of the bite often creates a situation in which officers find themselves physically engaged in the final mechanics of subduing the suspect.

■ Training exclusively for a spontaneous bite at the end of a track increases your risk of civil liability.

LAURA FOGERTY, TACTICAL PHOTOGRAPHY

Chapter 11: K9 Tracking — This Book Should Change Your K9 Life

In my experience, K9 teams who train exclusively for the spontaneous bite at the end of the track have implemented little K9 control in training. Typically, it's a case of let's track and search until we find the quarry, then we'll engage the quarry with overwhelming physical force. Failure to train for greater control when the quarry is located sets you up for two things: higher risk of a close-quarters gun battle that could be at point-blank range and, of course, increased risk of civil liability. My professional opinion is that K9 teams should broaden their K9 control to show that their tracking is not just one-dimensional when they encounter a hiding suspect.

Whether you have a bark-and-detain or a bite-and-hold training philosophy, your training should include a level of K9 control that does not always end with a bite on the quarry. The justification for that level of force should fall within the standard guidelines established by department policy and the laws that govern the use of force. No legal caveats allow the officer to circumvent the Fourth Amendment to the U.S. Constitution when it comes to tracking, and concern for officer safety does not provide a standard blanket of protection in training for the "spontaneous bite" at the end of a track. Your actions when using force will be measured by the objective-reasonableness standards set forth in the U.S. Supreme Court's 1989 *Graham v. Connor* decision.

Transitioning from one phase of training to the next

Your training records need to show your progression in tracking. Part of my job is to play devil's advocate for my fellow K9 handlers. What better way to prepare for a courtroom battle than to spar with an expert who will challenge everything you do? If I can make you look bad, then it's a sure bet that someone who gets paid $200 an hour will take you to the cleaners.

When I examine your tracking records, one of the things I'm looking for is the natural progression from simple training scenarios to a more robust, real-life tracking platform. Everyone starts out easy, and the defined mechanics of every track should be in your records. I want to know what techniques you used and see the gradual transition away

K9s In the Courtroom

■ Your tracking records should reflect a progression from simple training scenarios with constant stimulus to more robust, real-world tracks that include other officers and tactics.

from aids such as food drops, food drags, scuffed starting pads, agitation, and run-offs. I also want to see times when a track wasn't completed as successfully as you had planned for, and then I want to know how you set about recovering from that. Typically, an unsuccessful tracking exercise will be followed by a track that eliminates one or more stumbling blocks, so that the K9 finds success and pushes forward again.

Many times, I read training logs that are filled with the basic facts of the track and are void of any specific comments other than success or failure. I'm looking for additional facts that prove to everyone that you're advancing. The plateau, when it comes, is when you and your dog meet or exceed a definable level of acceptable performance. Such measures can and should be established in department policies and through an independent certification process by a recognizable association that provides K9 tracking certification.

Following are some of the transitions I look for in your records.
- Transitioning away from the constant use of food and food odors.
- Transitioning away from the constant stimulation of an aggressive quarry prior to the start of the track.
- Transitioning away from any other constant stimulus that typically defines the beginning stages of track-following.

Chapter 11: K9 Tracking — This Book Should Change Your K9 Life

- Implementation of aged tracks.
- Implementation of a variety of track layers.
- Implementation of a variety of track surfaces and environmental contaminants such as urban and rural settings, animals, humans, and distractions along the way.

Although the list of such things is limitless, I make my point with just a few examples in this book. There is a clear and convincing need to prove, through your training and K9 records, that you have mastered a plethora of difficulties and advanced the dog's tracking. To put this into clear perspective, you cannot convince people that you followed a real-world deployment track from point A to point B without proving that you were capable of doing so in training.

Broadening your capabilities

So you've mastered some advanced tracking in your training. You've aged the tracks and used multiple cross-contaminated tracks, evidence dropped along the way, aged hard surfaces, animal contamination, vehicle traffic, and multiple suspects. You feel successful, and you are. But you still have scenario-based work to do. You'll always work on the basic mechanics of tracking to maintain or advance the dog's abilities, but now you'll add cover officers and tactics to address various end games that the decoys will play out.

K9 control is paramount. You must work as a K9 handler first to ensure that the dog will not target members of the cover team while they are doing their jobs. The dog will experience extreme stress when you begin to incorporate multiple cover officers into the searching and tracking exercises. Consider beginning tracking training using one or two cover officers just to have early K9 habituation to their presence.

One of the simplest commands — the "down–stay" — begins to seem difficult for the dog to master. Imagine the moment of contact with a hiding decoy. Cover officers will be moving quickly to cover; they'll be yelling back and forth to one another and shouting verbal challenges to the quarry. In such situations, dogs are stimulated by three main senses: sight, hearing, and smell. If the dog hasn't acquired the decoy

K9s In the Courtroom

as a target using one of those three senses, guess who's drawing the dog's attention? The cover officers. They're now providing the dog with an overload of pressure. Your first response to this encounter should be to command the dog to "down." It takes practice, and lots of it, to get that right. This type of training is important so that if a civil suit is ever filed, one can clearly see from your training records that the deployment you were involved in was something you and your dog were fully capable of handling. Your training clearly mimicked the real-life event.

We cannot train for every imaginable real-life scenario, but we have few limits on our training scenarios. One day you might have both a criminal case and a civil case that stem from using the dog to track. If an expert is hired to review your performance, make sure your records show that the dog was capable of performing just as your written incident report says it did. If one of your cover officers gets bitten on a track and you've never trained with a full team of cover officers, or you've never exposed the dog to SWAT officers in full kit while maneuvering in a formation as you track, then it's reasonable to conclude that your dog's training was inadequate or insufficient.

The reasonable solution to any of those issues is the K9's exposure to steadily increasing environmental stress and the dog's gradual acceptance of handler commands. That profoundly simple philosophy is the foundation of every aspect of your patrol dog training. Yet numerous K9 handlers, trainers, and supervisors fail to understand the need — or even worse, fail to put forth the effort — to expand the dog's tolerance for environmental stress. Often we become mired in a cycle of repetitiveness: our training routines revolve around a series of tasks we must accomplish for certification or ones that require little K9 control. For example, unleashing the dog for a bite apprehension or a search-and-bite where we do little else but allow the dog to find and bite the suspect. We rush in with no regard for tactics to physically remove the dog from the bite or encourage the dog to aggressively locate the quarry. Our tactics in any search — not the least of which is high-risk tracking — should be carefully considered, well thought through, discussed with cover officers, and frequently trained with the

Chapter 11: K9 Tracking —This Book Should Change Your K9 Life

■ Your K9 should receive a steadily increasing exposure to stressful training scenarios.

dog so that the search team works and functions as a well-organized team. Taking full advantage of the team concept can reduce both the threat to human life and the risks associated with civil liability.

Angles of attack

I'm going to relate my own experience of how a plaintiff's experts will attempt to convince the court that you are the bad guy.

You use the dog to track someone down and that person gets bitten. You didn't see the dog bite him because the bad guy was concealing himself behind some underbrush or an obstacle. You saw behavioral changes in the dog prior to contact, which indicated that you were quite close to the suspect. Following are some of the questions that have arisen from such a case.

• Did you give a K9 warning before you started your track, giving the suspect an opportunity to surrender without being injured?
• If you knew you were close to the suspect based on the dog's behavior changes prior to the contact, why didn't you stop and give a K9 warning?
• Is your dog trained to bite people without being commanded to do so?

K9s In the Courtroom

• Does your dog bite for no reason when it finds a suspect at the end of a track?

As you can clearly see, those questions are quite direct and could be difficult to answer. Another legal attack will come from the way you start a track or differentiate between tracks. A case in point dealt with two men who attempted to steal a car in the middle of the night. As the men exited the car, an officer chased them into a wooded area. The officer quickly gave up the chase and moved to a nearby perimeter position along a highway. The K9 team arrived and the dog was directed to start its track at the last known sighting. The track ended as the K9 handler encountered an armed homeowner some distance away. In the confusion, the homeowner mistakenly took the officer for an armed trespasser and was subsequently shot by the officer. In the civil suit that followed, the plaintiff's K9 experts questioned, among other things, the validity of the dog's ability to track and the K9 handler's decision making. The claims were that the dog and handler were not properly trained and that the handler made poor decisions in deploying his dog. Here are some points of contention from the experts as they presented them to the courts.

• The dog could not have been on the suspects' track because there is no evidence to support the idea that the dog was ever on the right track. The handler should have taken a clean cotton swab and obtained an

■ The courts will question every aspect of your tracking deployment, from control of your dog to whether you gave a K9 warning before releasing the dog to bite a suspect.

Chapter 11: K9 Tracking —This Book Should Change Your K9 Life

odor sample from the inside of the car where the suspects had been.
• The dog could not have been on the suspects' track because there is no evidence to support the officer's assertion that the dog's track was started on the suspects' last known location, which was related to him by an officer who abandoned that post to hold a different perimeter point. There was no scene integrity and anyone could have walked through that area after the officer abandoned the location.
• The handler should have used his Taser or the dog to apprehend the homeowner, rather than shoot him.
• The officer reported that he shot with one hand while holding the dog's leash with the other. When asked what the dog was doing, he said jumping and bouncing up and down. That shows the handler had no control and that the dog was being disobedient to the point of being out of control, causing the homeowner to fear being attacked.
• No K9 warning was given before the handler entered the backyard in the middle of the night.
• No officers attempted to contact the homeowner by phone, by reverse 911, or by knocking on the door.

As you can see from those statements, we face a very real adversary in the judicial system and its experts are highly educated, experienced K9 people who can make a huge impression on people who know nothing about police dogs and often are suspicious of police officers and their tactics.

Aberrance could make you better, but it also could make you a legal target

Improving your deployment success could be measured in a number of ways other than apprehensions, number of arrests, or how you use your dog. Success could be seen as fewer officers accidentally bitten, fewer suspects injured, and greater K9 focus on the tasks of tracking or hunting than on the environment. Obviously, improvement happens through training and conditioning. Training is the antidote to unwanted K9 behavior. When I see one team excel far ahead of others within the same unit I have many questions, starting with, "What is one handler

doing to push himself ahead of the group?" The basic answer may simply be "hard work and persistence" — or is there more going on? Whether you are a handler, a K9 trainer, or a supervisor, you should ask the following critical questions:
• Does your K9 policy provide latitude for K9 handlers to use different training techniques to control the dog or to condition the dog to perform?
• Do all training techniques require prior department approval before they're used?
• Does your K9 policy define which types of training and deployment equipment each K9 team will use?
• Are there restrictions and limits to the list of equipment that handlers can use for training?
• Does the department need to approve equipment before handlers can use it in training or during deployments?

That is just a sample of the types of questions an attorney could pose during a court proceeding.

Your success is sometimes measured against the success of the others in your unit to form an imaginary baseline. Generally speaking, we all have a minimum standard to achieve through a certification process. The experts against you will look at the highest performing member of the unit and compare your team to the lowest performing member to make his point about discrepancies in training and supervision. As a plaintiff's expert, I would be asking the supervisor why, if he or she sees huge success in one K9 handler, wouldn't the same training be beneficial to everyone else in the unit?

Let's say for example that you use an e-collar and no one else does. That could be used as an example that you are operating outside the normal training regimen for your unit. Let's say that you track on a 30-foot lead and everyone else tracks on a 10-foot lead. You have tracked down a suspect and he gets bitten. One crazy assertion that could be made against you is that your aberrant behavior toward training and deployments caused you to use a 30-foot lead, which resulted in an unnecessary bite on the suspect. Because you allowed the dog too

Chapter 11: K9 Tracking — This Book Should Change Your K9 Life

much lead, the suspect was bitten. After all, everyone else in your unit uses a 10-foot lead. There must be a valid reason for that. How would your supervisor or trainer answer that assertion? In reality, it might be insignificant, but to members of a jury, discrepancies start to build up and the red herrings fly.

Please understand that I support everyone who goes outside the training bubble to seek higher education in dog training. I also support continuity and conformity. Just because a handler learns a new training technique doesn't mean that his trainer is off-course with what has been established as proper and successful in your agency's training regimen. Training and using techniques acquired outside of your department's knowledge and approval is ill-advised. Discuss the benefits of what you've learned with your trainers and supervisors but remember, you handle their dog for them.

Scenario-based training: the centerpiece of success and survival

I'm a huge advocate of scenario-based training, but in order to have success in any scenario, we must master the basic mechanics. A scenario is nothing more than bringing all the components of your K9 skills together in one focused operation. Nothing is more frustrating than poor performance in a training scenario. Let's face it, our egos live and

■ Discuss with your supervisors any unusual training techniques you may wish to use with your K9 prior to implementing them to avoid being accused of aberrant behavior in court.

K9s In the Courtroom

die with our dog's performance. Many handlers will shy away from training when they think they will look bad in front of other people, especially their peers.

I want you to understand that we fail most often in our scenario-based training *because we don't have control over our dog.* Failure is seldom because the dog didn't track well or search well, but rather because we spent more time exposing ourselves to deadly threats while trying to gain K9 compliance than anything else. Look at it this way, when the New York Yankees go to training, they don't play a full game. Those guys work on the fundamentals and the mechanics of running, batting, pitching, catching, etc. Our training should be the same. Work on the mechanics of K9 control. "Down" means "down-stay." When you give the dog a "down" command, nothing else around him should matter — nothing!

Once you expose the dog to more and more environmental stress and you have solid control, your other track and search mechanics will come together for the big game. Nothing is more frustrating to the SWAT team than to waste a day of training avoiding getting bitten or waiting until you've exhausted yourself trying to get the dog under control. Prepare yourself and your dog by practicing a lot without the SWAT team. Then come together for the scenario-based training as a full team, ready to play.

As an expert witness, I want to read about the scenarios that you've participated in. I want the details of your decision-making. Don't be afraid to make a mistake in training; you can safely learn from it. Practice doesn't make perfect, it makes permanent. Play the scenarios like they're real. In my tracking classes, I expose teams to many different end games in which the bad guy does a variety of things. The reason for that is simple: it forces the handler to make split-second decisions about a number of issues, any of which could result in deadly encounters in the real world. What's important is that once the decisions are made and the scenario ends, the entire episode is debriefed immediately within the group of cover officers and the handler. Decisions to engage the decoy with the dog, taking real cover, K9 control, movement, and cover officer

Chapter 11: K9 Tracking —This Book Should Change Your K9 Life

performances should all be discussed. Those quick debriefs show us the high and low points of our actions and decisions with regard to tactics and apprehensions. From them, the handler learns to make faster and better decisions under stress. The team also learns about its own proficiencies or the lack thereof.

Final thoughts on the most dangerous job in law enforcement

Statistically speaking, a K9 handler is seven times more likely than any other police officer in any other assignment to be involved in a lethal-force confrontation. That statistic alone should speak volumes about the courage and commitment each of you displays routinely throughout a single shift. Ours is a career filled with risky journeys that should always be traversed using our skillfully trained talents. But even more than that, our career is one that demands our fullest efforts and unwavering persistence in using our tactics so that we win every time. Trailing the path of the unknown behind a tethered police dog is truly an exercise in compromise. With each step forward, our lives hang in the balance.

    The rewards of the capture often are nothing more than the inner satisfaction of knowing that we were successful and didn't get hurt. Our reward should include the knowledge that what we've accomplished will follow through to a successful conviction with no civil litigation. Our mission isn't over when we put our dog back in the cruiser, it's usually just beginning. Make it a part of your K9 life to protect the hard work you've done on the street and in training with a solid understanding of your training techniques, the training you've done, and the way you deploy. Above all, go home at the end of each shift safely. Use tactics and cover when searching for suspects. Visit the firing range often with cover officers and your dog. Choose quality backup officers, train them, and teach them what's expected of them on tracks and searches. If you get into a bind, call one of us and ask us questions. Whether you need information about training, recordkeeping, testifying in court, or you need an expert K9 witness, you can contact the authors of this book for help.

■ ■ ■

Chapter 12

Detection Canine Recordkeeping

TO MOST PEOPLE, DETECTION CANINES are a little mysterious. People don't understand how K9s can detect the amount of odor they do, nor do they understand how K9s can be trained to detect those odors. That makes it challenging to convince people of K9 reliability. A properly trained drug detection canine can provide probable cause during a criminal investigation. When detection canines are used to establish probable cause in a criminal investigation, courts must decide K9 reliability.

No other law-enforcement canine discipline is as critiqued as detection canines. No other law-enforcement canine discipline is as litigated as detection canines. No other law-enforcement canine discipline is as controversial as detection canines. All of that criticism, litigation, and controversy focuses on the detection canine's reliability. Essentially the question is, "Does your detection canine find the target odor only or exclusively?"

Defense attorneys have argued and will argue that all canines are unreliable. They will use information about canine training they have learned at various conferences, and they will use canine trainers, animal behaviorists, and veterinarians to attempt to prove your dog is unreliable.

Defense attorneys also will attempt to convince a judge that detection dogs find odors other than the target odor, are influenced by their environment and handler, or are poorly trained. Sometimes they will argue all of those points at the same time. To do so, they will challenge the handler's knowledge about training and maintaining a reliable detection canine. They will want proof that the dog was trained properly and

Chapter 12: Detection Canine Recordkeeping

is currently being trained properly. Testimony from a law-enforcement officer that he or she does the proper training is no longer enough. Documentation of such training is essential to proving the case.

This chapter discusses the various ways a defense attorney may attack a drug detection canine in court and the documentation needed to prove a K9 team's reliability in court.

Are written records needed?

The need for written records has been indisputable since 1994 in *United States v. Florez*, 871 F. Supp. 1411 (1994), in which the court stated, "Where records are not kept or are insufficient to establish the dog's reliability, an alert by such a dog is much like hearsay from an anonymous informant."

The quote taken from this case focuses on two things: "not kept" and "are insufficient to establish the dog's reliability." Not only must you keep records, the records must have a sufficient amount of information to establish the dog's reliability. If you fail in either of those two points, the alert/indication from your team is "much like hearsay from an anonymous informant."

A tip from an anonymous informant will not provide probable cause in a criminal investigation. The dog alert/indication is then useless to the criminal case. In the *Florez* case, the court felt that training records for K9 Bobo were not sufficiently kept to prove the dog's reliability (*Florez*, 871 F. Supp at 1422). Indeed, defense counsel brought up four instances in which Bobo alerted and no drugs were found, but which were not among the incident reports produced. That highlights the impossible task of remembering a dog's daily activities, including false positives and accurate alerts without documentation.

Because the defense was able to find cases in which K9 Bobo alerted/indicated that were not recorded in the canine records, the veracity of the records in totality was questionable. The court felt that because a handler cannot remember all of a dog's daily activities, including false positives and accurate alerts, records must be accurately kept, and when that is not done, their credibility is questionable.

K9s In the Courtroom

■ Handlers sometimes think a defense attorney challenge will come only if a large amount of drugs are found, but that is not the case: even small finds may be questioned in court.

Most recently in *Florida v. Harris,* the U.S. Supreme Court wrote that probable cause can be established by the indication/alert of a certified and trained drug detection canine. The court further explained that although it believed that field performance records were of little import to proving or disproving the dog's alert/indication, they still could be a factor for the court to consider. The U.S. Supreme Court wrote that a better evaluation of a dog's reliability would be an assessment of training and certification. That opinion was based on the inability to know for sure whether drug odor was present in real-life cases, as opposed to the controlled and known setting of a training exercise or certification.

The court felt that law enforcement would have no motivation to have poorly trained dogs. A poorly trained dog would provide inaccurate information, waste time and manpower, and potentially place officers in a dangerous situation.

The two cases we've discussed are opposite in many ways, yet are the same in the most important points. Both cases focus on the train-

Chapter 12: Detection Canine Recordkeeping

ing of the dog and handler and emphasize the defense's ability to use an expert to evaluate the canine team's training and certification. Proof of the dog team's ability lies in the handler's testimony and documentation of the team's training methods and performance.

Defense attorneys will issue court-approved subpoenas for a dog team's training and deployment records. In those subpoenas, they will ask for many other pieces of information as well. Following are a few of the things a defense team may ask for along with an explanation of why they are asking for them.

Subpoena requests and requirements

Subpoena paragraph: *Any and all records in the possession of your agency on all dogs currently used by your agency in the investigation of drug offenses.*

The defense is asking for all records of all dog teams to compare the other teams in the agency with the one that is involved in the case. They may compare the performance of the dogs in training and in the field.

Subpoena paragraph: *All records and or documents (including video) that pertain, relate to, or describe the training of the drug dog team. Records or documents must be from the time the team was formed to include the initial training. (Many times the records start in the field and all dogs must receive training before working in the field.)*

Attacking the abilities and qualifications of the trainer of the dog and handler, along with the training methods used, is a tactic used by the defense; also, evaluating the performance of the dog team during the initial training course.

The basic information needed for training records is not extensive. Many people keep much more detailed information, but the following would be the minimum amount of information needed:
- Date
- Time
- Location of training
- Type of exercise environment (vehicle, open area, package, etc.)

K9s In the Courtroom

- Length of exercise (time started to time completed)
- Drug substance (marijuana, cocaine, etc.)
- Drug packaging protocol (varying packaging)
- Amount of drug (varying quantities)
- Distracters/Proofing
- Controlled negatives (blanks, unknown to handler)
- Comments

Subpoena paragraph: *All records, reports, and documentation to include video recordings that relate to the field use of the drug dog, including statements of others who observed the event and information about the event.*

Field-use or deployment logs will be asked for and should be kept. The minimum information handlers should keep follows:
- Date
- Time
- Location
- Type of environment (vehicle, package, open area, etc.)
- No Indication/Alert
- Indication/Alert — drugs found
- Indication/Alert — no drugs found (verification: corroborating information that supports the indication/alert)
- Indication/Alert — no drugs found and no verification
- Currency inspected (alert or no alert)

Subpoena paragraph: *All departmental or organizational policies, rules, directives, memos, operating orders, and operating procedures governing or related to the training of the drug detection dog, including*
- *Certification standards,*
- *Minimum accepted proficiency,*
- *Reliability standards, and*
- *Minimum allowable training time for dog team each month.*

Every department has a *Policy and Procedures Manual* and should have a section in that manual for using detection canines. In the

Chapter 12: Detection Canine Recordkeeping

preceding paragraph, the defense attorney is looking for the standards the agency requires each team to reach and how the agency evaluates whether the team reached that standard. Defense attorneys have attacked certifications in the following ways.
- Conducted yearly
- Evaluation of behavior change to other odors (packaging materials, novel odors)
- Controlled negatives (blank areas, number of hides/finds unknown to handler)
- Must find all drug odors canine is trained to find (in varying amounts).
- Search time should vary (to show that the canine can work varying amounts of time).
- Varying exercise environments (vehicles, packages, open areas, etc.).

If your certification does not test for such items, you should provide those training exercises in your weekly training.

Policy and procedures should articulate the monthly minimum training time allowed for dog teams. Weekly training should be required, and handlers should be mandated to attend unless excused by supervision. Policy should provide a general goal or intended purpose for the weekly training.

Subpoena paragraph: *All departmental or organizational policies, rules, directives, memos, operating orders, and operating procedures governing or relating to the field use of a drug detector dog, including the following:*
- *recording methods,*
- *directions for conducting various tasks,*
- *random searches of vehicles (luggage, packages, etc.), and*
- *singled out (vehicles, luggage, packages, etc.).*

Deployments should be recorded using a standard methodology that each handler follows. Policy should dictate what form of recordkeeping system is used, and that the records are kept up-to-date and reviewed periodically by a supervisor. Policy and procedures also should dictate how long each team's records will be kept.

K9s In the Courtroom

Defense attorneys have attacked handlers' deployment methods for inspecting random areas and singled-out environments. It is advisable to provide general guidance for handlers to follow when deploying their canines. The handler should deploy the canine in compliance with policy and procedures — as well as local, state, and federal laws — in a manner that will attain the highest level of proficiency of detection. Standards should be established through a drug detection canine training program.

Policy and procedures should explain in general terms the permitted uses of detection canines, such as sniffing
- currency for forfeiture proceedings,
- buildings,
- luggage,
- vehicles or other conveyances,
- objects or open areas, and
- persons (only passive, single-purpose canines).

Policy should also state who is in charge of deploying the canine on scene. Because of the knowledge required to determine whether a deployment is legal — as well as the most advantageous method of deployment — the handler should control the scene and make the decision about when and how the dog is deployed.

Subpoena paragraph: *All training of the dog team's supervisor that relates to the training, use, and management of drug detector dog teams.*

The supervisor of a canine unit should have a working knowledge of
- policy and procedures,
- daily and weekly training,
- intended purpose of training,
- whether teams are following policy and procedures,
- minimum standards and certifications,
- recordkeeping methods and review,
- use logs,
- training logs,

Chapter 12: Detection Canine Recordkeeping

- utilization methods and standards,
- capabilities and limitations,
- what the canine will and won't find, and
- permitted and prohibited uses.

Subpoena paragraph: *All news articles, recordings, videos, tapes, etc., about this drug dog team.*
Defense attorneys will be looking for any and all information they can find about your canine. A defense expert can interpret videotapes in many ways, and that is something they will focus on.

■ If your dog's indication was used to support a search warrant, defense attorneys will want to check the results of that warrant.

K9s In the Courtroom

Subpoena paragraph: *Last date of certification or validation testing to include evaluator's written notes or comment, and videotapes.*
The defense will confirm with the certifying body that the dog team is certified. The defense will look for any noted weaknesses or errors during the certification. The defense has attacked the certifying body's criteria for certification.

Subpoena paragraph: *List all drugs the dog is trained to detect, to include synthetic drugs.*
Not all drug dogs are trained to find the same odors. Provide a section in the policy and procedures manual that delineates what odors the agency dogs are trained to find. If pseudo odors are used, the policy can articulate the permitted uses of pseudo and actual controlled substances.

Subpoena paragraph: *Define the dog's final response:*
- *Aggressive*
- *Passive*

When answering that question, we suggest that you define the dog's response completely, from initial behavior change through final response.

Subpoena paragraph: *Medical records for dog*
Studies have been done on commonly used drugs and illnesses that may inhibit the canine's olfactory capabilities.

Subpoena paragraph: *Police reports, warrants, and laboratory reports that relate to the use of this detector dog team.*
If your dog's indication was used to support a search warrant, defense attorneys will want to check the results of that warrant.

Subpoena paragraph: *Laboratory analysis or field test results on all target odors found as a result of this dog's response in real-world searches.*
The defense will compare the test results to your indications/alerts. For

Chapter 12: Detection Canine Recordkeeping

PACKTRACK

■ Recordkeeping software such as PACKTRACK helps handlers fill in the gaps and produce a more comprehensive, and court-savvy, training record.

example, a narcotics detective asked a deputy sheriff to have his K9 sniff a vehicle. The K9 deputy responded to the traffic stop and inspected the vehicle's exterior. The K9 deputy observed an indication from his dog that a target odor was present in the vehicle. The K9 handler did not place the K9 into the suspect vehicle; instead, the narcotics detective searched the vehicle's interior. The narcotics detective located a spoon containing what he believed to be and field-tested positive as methamphetamine. That spoon and substance was tested at the agency's lab and was found to be something other than an illegal drug. The defense attorney sent the K9 deputy and the county's criminal defense lawyer's association a letter explaining that the K9 had indicated to something other than the target odor. That was done to discredit the dog and handler.

Handlers sometimes think a defense attorney challenge will come only if a large amount of drugs are found, but that is not true. Most challenges occur in situations where what would be considered a small amount of drugs are found but, if convicted, the suspect would have much to lose. In the *Florida v. Harris* case, only methamphetamine precursor drugs were located and the subject was charged with possession of pseudoephedrine and other drugs.

Recordkeeping is a tedious but necessary part of canine training. If you wait to improve your recordkeeping until you receive a notice of motion to suppress or a subpoena asking for information similar to what was listed in this chapter, it will be too late. You must improve your records now and plan as if your records will be challenged every time you deploy your dog.

■ ■ ■

Chapter 13

Dog Reliability

Florida v. Harris

In 2013, the United States Supreme Court ruled on the issue of dog reliability in its opinion *Florida v. Harris*. February 19, 2013, will go down in dog-handler history as the day that the U.S. Supreme Court voted 9–0 to reverse the Florida Supreme Court's decision on the issue of narcotics K9 reliability. The Court found that the mandatory requirement of field reports and usage logs, along with the percentage calculation of an error factor, need not be mandated in court in order for the state to establish a dog's reliability related to a finding of probable cause to search. This chapter analyzes the *Harris* decision and how it has affected narcotics dog handlers across the country.

Justice Kagan, writing for a unanimous Supreme Court, stated, "the decision below [the Florida Supreme Court's previous ruling] treats records of a dog's field performance as the gold standard in evidence, when in most cases they have relatively limited import. Errors may abound in such records. If a dog on patrol fails to alert to a car containing drugs, the mistake usually will go undetected because the officer will not initiate a search. Field data thus may not capture a dog's false negatives. Conversely (and more relevant here), if the dog alerts to a car in which the officer finds no narcotics, the dog may not have made a mistake at all. The dog may have detected substances that were too well hidden or present in quantities too small for the officer to locate. Or the dog may have smelled the residual odor of drugs previously in the vehicle or on the driver's person. Field data thus may markedly overstate a dog's real false positives. By contrast, those inaccuracies, in

Chapter 13: Dog Reliability

either direction, do not taint records of a dog's performance in standard training and certification settings. There, the designers of an assessment know where drugs are hidden and where they are not and so where a dog should alert and where [it] should not. The better measure of a dog's reliability thus comes away from the field, in controlled testing environments."

That quote captured the main thrust of the police dog handler's position that training records and/or annual independent certification by a recognized organization truly are the best measure of a canine's reliability because, unlike field work, training and certification take place in a controlled setting. The High Court agreed.

The Court went on to illustrate this position, saying, "evidence of a dog's satisfactory performance in a certification or training program can itself provide sufficient reason to trust [its] alert. If a bona fide organization has certified a dog after testing [its] reliability in a controlled setting, a court can presume (subject to any conflicting evidence offered) that the dog's alert provides probable cause to search.

"The same is true, even in the absence of formal certification, if the dog has recently and successfully completed a training program that evaluated [its] proficiency in locating drugs. After all, law enforcement units have their own strong incentive to use effective training and certification programs, because only accurate drug-detection dogs enable officers to locate contraband without incurring unnecessary risks or wasting limited time and resources."

Harris eliminates the misnomer "false alert"

The Court's decision is a big victory for handlers all across the country, because the traditional defense attorney rhetoric definition of "false alert" has been quashed. In its opinion, the Court recognized that just because a dog alerts to an area where no drugs are found does not mean, in and of itself, that the dog was wrong — or as many unenlightened defense attorneys used to say, "false." To be honest, the ruling states that certification is not truly necessary if your initial training and weekly training are up to snuff. The Court found that even in the absence of formal certification, it is sufficient if the dog has recently and successfully completed a training program that evaluated its proficiency in locating drugs.

The defense attack

Therefore, contrary to popular belief, the opinion does not mean that the handler no longer needs to keep good records. Accurate and complete records are still essential to overcoming a challenge to your dog's reliability in court. The defense attorney can still hire an expert witness to review your records in an attempt to discredit your dog. The main area of attack will now focus on the dog's initial training. The attack could come in the form of the computer theory "garbage in, garbage out." That is to say, if the dog was first trained improperly and weekly maintenance training serves only to reinforce the original training, then the argument could be made that your dog is not reliable.

The second area of attack mostly likely will come from a defense expert saying that your certification test was not satisfactory. The expert will choose to pick on the procedures in place for certification, or the style or manner of testing used. The defense also may question who the judges were that passed your dog and their relationship to you and your dog. Areas of contention may include issues such as, "were the organization's rules followed?" However, if your dog was trained properly, is currently maintained properly, and has an annual narcotics certification from a bona-fide group, the *Harris* case will help you in court.

Because of the *Harris* ruling, the days of calculating the percentages of alert with a real find of drugs in the field, versus the percentages of alert with no finding of drugs in the field, is unnecessary for court. The Court went on to say, "In short, a probable-cause hearing focusing on a dog's alert should procede much like any other. The court should allow the parties to make their best case, consistent with the usual rules of criminal procedure. And the court should then evaluate the proffered evidence to decide what all the circumstances demonstrate. If the State has produced proof from controlled settings that a dog performs reliably in detecting drugs, and the defendant has not contested that

Chapter 13: Dog Reliability

showing, then the Court should find probable cause.

"If, in contrast, the defendant has challenged the State's case (by disputing the reliability of the dog overall or of a particular alert), then the court should weigh the competing evidence. In all events, the Court should not prescribe, as the Florida Supreme Court did, an inflexible set of evidentiary requirements. The question is whether all the facts surrounding a dog's alert, viewed through the lens of common sense, would make a reasonably prudent person think that a search would reveal contraband or evidence of a crime. A sniff is up to snuff when it meets that test."

Cases after *Harris*

In the case of *State of Kansas v. Brewer,* 305 P.3d 676 (July 12, 2013), the state appeals court found when applying the *Harris* ruling that, "Although it appears that no Kansas courts have explicitly addressed the issue, courts in a majority of jurisdictions either have minimized or rejected real-world deployment records as material evidence of a K9's reliability, in part because of a K9's ability to detect residual odor even where drugs are not found. We side with the majority of courts that have found that it is immaterial to use a real-world false positive rate to challenge a K9's reliability, because a K9 can detect residual odor even after drugs have been removed from a vehicle. Based on the evidence presented in Brewer's case that the K9 was properly certified at the time of the exterior air sniff and that the K9 had undergone the required continued training, we conclude the district court properly relied on the K9 alert in finding that the officer had probable cause to conduct a warrantless vehicle search."

Likewise in the case of *United States v. Burrows,* on May 1, 2014, the United States Court of Appeals for the Eleventh Circuit found as follows applying the *Harris* reliability standard: "*Burrows* also contends that the drug dog's alert did not establish probable cause because the dog was trained in detecting residual odors of drugs no longer present in a vehicle. *Burrows'* argument is that because the drug dog was trained in residual odor detection, and because the minivan was a rental, the dog's alert was 'not probative,' as it was 'likely' that the dog 'alerted to drug odors in the car caused by someone else's drug use.' "

In *Harris,* the Supreme Court addressed a "residual odor" argument similar to *Burrows*'s. It stated that, "[i]n the usual case, the mere chance that the substance might no longer be at the location does not matter; a well-trained dog's alert establishes a fair probability — all that is required for probable cause — that either drugs or evidence of a drug crime . . . will be found." The fact that Burrows did not own the car he was driving did not make the case unusual.

Therefore, keep up the good work and keep maintaining good training and deployment records, and *Florida v. Harris* will help you carry the day in court in terms of dog reliability.

■ ■ ■

Chapter 14

Dogs Sniffing Houses and Apartments

Florida v. Jardines

The canine community was not as fortunate in the results in the case of *Florida v. Jardines,* or as I affectionately call it, Dog Sniffing Houses. In a close five-to-four vote, the United States Supreme Court held that the front porch of a home, which was the location where the law-enforcement officials used a drug-sniffing dog to investigate an unverified tip that marijuana was being grown in the home, was part of the curtilage of the home and therefore was a constitutionally protected area for Fourth Amendment purposes. But introducing a trained police dog to explore the area around the home in hopes of discovering incriminating evidence is something else. There is no customary invitation to do *that.* An invitation to engage in canine forensic investigation assuredly does not inhere in the very act of hanging a knocker. Law enforcement officers' use of a drug-sniffing dog on the front porch of the home, to investigate an unverified tip that marijuana was being grown in the home, was a trespassory invasion of the curtilage which constituted a "search" for Fourth Amendment purposes.

As I write this next paragraph, I know most of you officers are going to be scratching your heads, but please do not shoot the messenger. The High Court found that when a police officer approaches a door and knocks to merely speak to the resident, it is lawful. Therefore, the traditional "knock-and-talk" method is still a viable technique and not a trespass; but when you approach the front door with a trained narcotics dog at your side, it somehow becomes a trespass. Don't ask me to explain it. The four dissenting justices do not understand it either.

K9s In the Courtroom

The practical application is that you can still use a dog on a house, but you must first secure a search warrant (what I refer to as a "sniff warrant") before you put the dog on the house. That means, in short, that if you have three or four factors that establish that the house is being used has a grow house, write a search warrant exclusively for the sole purpose of sniffing the exterior of the house. When the judge signs the warrant, you now can sniff the house. If the dog alerts, then write the second warrant with the same three or four factors and now include the dog alert and you should be able to gain entry into the house using the second search warrant. But law enforcement can no longer — either randomly or simply based upon a tip — put a dog on a house to sniff it.

The *Jardines* ruling was based on the theory that the officer with the dog "trespassed" onto the curtilage of the home. Therefore, the Court would seem to be saying that if the dog were used in a common area (a hallway where every guest has the right to be), then use of the dog would be allowed. In plain language, I read the case to hold that a dog *can still be used* from a common hallway in a hotel or motel. Bottom line: when running your dog in a hotel/motel situation, ask yourself these questions: "Am I trespassing? Or am I lawfully present in a common area open to the general public?" If the answer to the second question is "yes," you can use the dog.

Apartment use after *Jardines*

What is going on with dog sniffs on apartments? We are beginning to see how *Jardines* will affect sniffs on apartment doors from common hallways. Court decisions are being made in favor of law enforcement, but it is too early in the overall litigation process to declare victory.

One of the most recent relevant cases is *U.S. v. Penaloza-Romero*, 2013 WL 5472283 D.Minn, September 30, 2013. Factually, the defendant's phone was pinged and investigators began surveillance. Law enforcement followed the defendant to an apartment building on Colfax Avenue in Minneapolis. A mailbox was identified as being rented in the name of Padilla–Valle. Information received by law enforcement identified Padilla–Valle as part of a separate criminal organization with close

Chapter 14: Dogs Sniffing Houses and Apartments

ties to the defendant. They determined that the defendant was staying at the Colfax apartment.

Law enforcement contacted the manager of the apartment building. The police told the manager that they would like to enter the building to perform a dog sniff of the apartments. The manager consented and opened the door. The sniff occurred in the common hallway of the building. The canine alerted to the presence of narcotics after sniffing the seam of the apartment door. The manager confirmed that Ernesto Padilla–Valle rented the apartment. A search warrant was issued based upon the dog sniff, the landlord's confirmation that the apartment was leased to Padilla–Valle, and a CI's identification of a photo of Padilla–Valle as being involved in distributing methamphetamine.

The defendant first argued that the dog sniff of the hallway of the apartment building was a search pursuant to the Fourth Amendment and therefore required a warrant. The defendant based his argument on *Florida v. Jardines,* 133 S.Ct. 1409 (2013). In *Jardines,* police walked a dog to the front porch. The dog sensed drug odors and began to trace them, eventually sniffing the base of the front door and determining that to be the odor's strongest point. The Court observed that the evidence was gathered on the house's curtilage, a constitutionally protected area. Because of that, the Court examined whether the investigation was achieved through an unlicensed intrusion. The first question to ask is whether a person is "on the constitutionally protected extension of the home."

The defendant's reliance on *Jardines* is misplaced because it cannot be said that the common hallway of the apartment building was curtilage. The defendant relied on *United States v. Dunn,* 480 U.S. 294 (1987). The court in *Dunn* identified four factors relevant to determining curtilage: (1) the proximity of the area claimed to be curtilage to the home, (2) whether the area is included within an enclosure surrounding the home, (3) the nature of the uses to which the area is put, and (4) the steps taken by the resident to protect the area from observation by people passing by.

Applying those factors from *Dunn* does not support finding a common hallway to be curtilage. The common hallway is close to the apartment in question and also within the enclosure surrounding it, meeting the first two factors. The third factor, however, weighs against a finding of curtilage. The nature of a common hallway is not a corridor used for intimate activities, but rather to permit residents of the building ingress from and egress to the street. The fourth factor also weighs against a finding that a common hallway is curtilage. Although passersby may not be able to see the hallway, those with whom the resident shares the hallway can still view the activities of the resident while he is in the hallway. Indeed, an apartment resident most likely would not be permitted to shield his activities in the hallway from the other residents, as they have the same right to access it that he does

Furthermore, it is well settled in the Eighth Circuit "that there exists no 'generalized expectation of privacy in the common areas of an apartment building.'" *United States v. Brooks,* 645 F.3d 971, 976 (8th Cir. 2011). In that case, the dog sniff occurred in a common hallway of an apartment building. Accordingly, because the search at issue did not occur on a constitutionally protected extension of the home, *Jardines* is inapposite.

Another federal court ruling

In *U.S. v. Mathews,* 2013 WL 5781566 D.Minn. (Oct. 2013), the federal district court held, "The court concludes that the positive indication for narcotics based upon the dog sniff was sufficient in itself to establish probable cause for issuance of the search warrant. See *United States v. Scott,* 610 F.3d 1009, (8th Cir.2010). The defendant had no reasonable expectation of privacy extending into a common hallway of the apartment building. The presence of police officers with a drug detection canine was not a violation of the defendant's Fourth Amendment rights, and evidence obtained by dog sniff was not unlawfully obtained. The defendant likens the apartment hallway to the front porch of a residence and argues that the common area is curtilage, to which the resident's Fourth Amendment rights attach under *Florida v. Jardines,* 133 S.Ct. 1409 (2013).

Chapter 14: Dogs Sniffing Houses and Apartments

■ The courts have found that a positive indication for narotics based on a dog sniff of a common area is sufficient to establish probable cause for the issuance of a search warrant.

"The court does not agree that the apartment hallway is curtilage to the home. Although the hall area is proximate to the apartment residence and is included within the structure, the hall is merely a passageway and it offers neither privacy from the view of neighbors nor a right to restrict another person's appropriate use of the hallway. See *United States v. Dunn*. There is no 'generalized expectation of privacy in the common areas of an apartment building.' See *United States v. Brooks* (quoting *United States v. McCaster,* 193 F.3d 930, 933 (8th Cir.1999). A clear qualitative distinction exists between the expectation of privacy to be enjoyed on the front porch of one's home and the protection from intrusion that may apply to a hallway in apartment building. The Fourth Amendment protection afforded under *Jardines* does not reach far enough to overrule *United States v. Scott,* and *Jardines* does not render the dog sniff evidence in this matter unlawful for purposes of establishing probable cause."

State Supreme Court and *Jardines*

The Supreme Court of North Dakota, in their opinion of *State v. Nguyen*, 841 N.W.2d 676, N.D. 2013. (Dec. 26, 2013), held that the defendant did not have a reasonable expectation of privacy in the common hallways of his apartment building, and thus entry of the hallways by law-enforcement officers was not a search under the Fourth Amendment, even though the entrance to the building was locked and secured, and the officers were technical trespassers in the hallways. The entrance was designed to provide security for the tenants rather than to provide privacy in the common hallways; the common hallways were available for the use of tenants and their guests, the landlord and his agents, and others having legitimate reason to be on the premises; and the defendant could not have excluded individuals from the hallways.

The decision in *Jardines* appears to be limited by the courts to actual homes. Apartments, townhouses, condos, or motels, so far have been seen as having common hallways or common areas that are open to all other residents and their guests. Because those areas are common to others, they are available to officers and their dogs. Therefore, like the residents and their friends, police are not trespassers. Consequently, *Jardines* would not apply. On dog sniffing houses issues, remember to always ask yourself this question: "Am I lawfully present where I stand, or am I a trespasser?" If you are present where all others have the right to be, then you and your narcotics dog should be good to go.

■ ■ ■

Chapter 15

Checkpoints: What to Do or What Not to do

CHECKPOINTS HAVE BEEN A POPULAR and useful tool for law-enforcement officers for many years. They help locate law violators that normally would go undetected. The most common checkpoints are associated with two main areas: (1) driving under the influence of drugs or alcohol or (2) vehicle safety inspections that check for common equipment violations.

Real checkpoints

In 1998, the City of Indianapolis, Indiana, attempted to expand the checkpoint usage into the area of narcotics-interdiction checkpoints. Police officers would walk their trained narcotics detection dogs around the exterior of each car stopped at the city's drug checkpoint. The city operated six roadblock-style checkpoints between August and November 1998. In total, 1,161 vehicles were stopped resulting in 104 arrests. Fifty-five arrests were for narcotics-related offenses, and 49 arrests were for crimes unrelated to narcotics. To put motorists on notice, signs were posted that read "Narcotics checkpoint __ mile ahead, narcotics K9 in use, be prepared to stop."

Cases that were challenged went all the way to the United States Supreme Court. The issue was decided under a case titled *City of Indianapolis v. Edmond,* 531 U.S. 32, 121 S. Ct. 447, 147 L. Ed. 2d 333 (2000). The Supreme Court held that a checkpoint designed to protect the country's border in order to intercept illegal aliens, sobriety checkpoints aimed at removing drunk drivers from the roadways, or checkpoints that promote highway safety interests are all permissible

■ A narcotics K9 sniff of a vehicle can legally occur any time between the begining of a valid traffic stop and the time when the officer hands the driver of the vehicle a citation.

practices for law enforcement. However, the high court went on to find that a checkpoint designed for the primary purpose of ferreting out general criminal activity, such as transporting narcotics, violates the Fourth Amendment of the United States Constitution.

Although the Supreme Court shut down the operation of using checkpoints to detect narcotics-related crimes, they did not disavow the use of dogs at checkpoints. When a checkpoint is established for one of the lawful primary purposes previously listed, a trained narcotics canine can be on scene and used for its unique talents if the need arises. What one must understand is the meaning of the governing language of *primary purpose.* If, for example, at a D.U.I. checkpoint, an officer has a car stopped for inspection due to the driver exhibiting signs of impairment, it is still lawful to run a dog around the exterior of the car to attempt to detect the odor of narcotics. That is lawful because the checkpoint's primary purpose is to detect drunk drivers and not general crime. The fact that a dog may be used on a few cars at the

Chapter 15: Checkpoints: What to Do or What Not to Do

checkpoint does not convert the primary purpose of the checkpoint itself.

Notice that I specified that the narcotics canine was used on a *few* cars at the checkpoint: not on every car that was stopped, not even on 50 percent of the cars stopped. The dog should be used only when the facts and circumstances dictate that the deployment is appropriate, and the number of deployments should be a low number or percentage related to the other cars that are stopped associated with the checkpoint's primary purpose. Also, the majority of the officers on scene should be from the traffic division, not narcotics detectives, because if you were to have 30 drug detectives and 9 traffic cops working the checkpoint, it would be hard to argue that the primary purpose of the checkpoint is D.U.I. detection or vehicle safety. Common sense would militate against naming the checkpoint "Operation Drug Pipeline." That would be an excellent tip-off of a narcotics checkpoint. Instead, maybe "Operation Highway Safety" would be a better choice.

Fake checkpoints

One must understand that once a car is stopped, detained, or diverted for inspection at a checkpoint, the car and its occupants have been "seized" for the purpose of the Fourth Amendment. But what if the car was never stopped, detained, or diverted for inspection? Then the Constitutional protections against unreasonable searches would not apply to the car or its occupants. The roadblock then constitutes a fake checkpoint, or what is commonly referred to as the checkpoint or roadblock ruse.

That ruse, trick, con, scam, hoax, ploy, or stunt, however it is labeled, is completely legal. This is how it works: *United States v. Martinez,* 358 F. 3d 1005 (8th Circuit Court of Appeals 2004) held that a police officer's use of deceptive highway signs indicating a drug enforcement checkpoint was ahead, when in fact none really existed, did not render an otherwise valid traffic stop illegal because there truly was no drug checkpoint. Therefore, no cars were actually being seized for inspection, and only the cars the officers witnessed as committing valid traffic violations to avoid a nonexistent checkpoint were being stopped.

The Eighth Circuit Court of Appeals found that the Defendant Martinez' arguments that (1) his traffic violation cannot be considered a valid basis for the stop because it was the direct result of an illegal checkpoint, and (2) the drugs [found] are inadmissible because they were the indirect result of an illegal checkpoint are foreclosed by the court's conclusion that there was no illegal checkpoint in this case." (*Martinez,* supra at 1009.) In this case, signs were used that read "DRUG ENFORCEMENT CHECKPOINT AHEAD, ONE-FOURTH MILE" and "DRUG DOG IN USE." Such signs are fine as long as there is no checkpoint ahead. There is no law against posting the signs, and if the drug courier or trafficker reads them and is observed committing a valid traffic violation in order to avoid what he or she believes is an active drug checkpoint with a trained narcotics detection canine in use, shame on them. Detectives should feel free to set signs out on a road with a double yellow line going right down the middle of the road. If, after reading fake checkpoint signs, the driver makes a U-turn and crosses over those double yellow lines, they can be legally stopped! An illegal U-turn to avoid a fake drug checkpoint is merely a traffic violation.

When you combine the tactic of the fake checkpoint with the United States Supreme Court's ruling in *Whren v. United States,* 517 U.S. 806, 116 S.Ct. 1769, 135 L.Ed.2d 89 (1996), any valid traffic violation provides an officer with probable cause to stop the offending vehicle and issue a citation. The court in *Whren* found, under the Fourth Amendment, the officer's reasons for stopping the vehicle are immaterial and the stop is lawful when an officer has probable cause to believe that a traffic offense has occurred. The legal standard is whether an officer could have stopped the car for the infraction. Therefore, seeing a traffic infraction being committed by a driver whom you think might also be carrying drugs in his or her car is legally permissible.

The dog handler needs to be nearby because the regular rules and timeframes for using the dog still apply. The dog handler still must use

Chapter 15: Checkpoints: What to Do or What Not to Do

his or her trained canine partner within a reasonable timeframe that it would take the stopping officer to write a ticket. During the course of issuing the ticket for the illegal U-turn, in our example, the canine alerts; bingo, now you have probable cause to search the vehicle and seize the drugs that, thanks to the checkpoint ruse, are now admissible in court. The drug trafficker and his defense attorney probably will feel that he and his client were fooled into committing the traffic violation that led to his arrest. Gee, that's really too bad, don't you think?

■ ■ ■

Chapter 16

Dogs Jumping Into Cars

WORKING A NARCOTICS DOG CAN BE REWARDING and frustrating at the same time. No matter how well a handler works and trains with his or her canine on a regular basis, things do not always go as planned. Dogs do have a mind of their own. Their hunt and prey drives are put to the test every day. This chapter focuses on dogs' natural instinct to find the source of the odor they are trained to detect.

At a lawful traffic stop, a handler will deploy his or her canine partner before the traffic ticket is completed. The general rule of thumb is no longer than approximately 15 minutes from the initial stop of the defendant's vehicle. During this deployment, the handler presents the vehicle to the dog for inspection by exterior sniff. During the exterior sniff of the vehicle, the dog is trained to scent-discriminate and to seek the odor of one of the narcotics it has been trained to find. A handler has the ability to visually watch his or her dog for those first indicators that the dog is "on" or "in" odor. A head throw, rapid breathing patterns, stiff tail, becoming more focused, hair standing, to name a few, are all signs of a change in behavior indicating that the dog has found odor but may not be at source yet — or at least as close to source as possible.

At a typical traffic stop, the officer's canine would sit, stare, bite, or scratch at the closed door, window, hood, or trunk seams. But what if that door, window, hood, or trunk were open? What would happen legally to the search in court, on a motion to suppress, if in an effort to find source odor the well-trained canine partner instinctively put its nose through the window or — better yet — leaped into the car through the opening in an attempt to locate the source of the narcotics odor? Would

Chapter 16: Dogs Jumping Into Cars

that be an illegal entry into the car by the dog before its final alert or trained final response without cause?

No aiding the dog

Several major factors come into play when answering that question. First, the open door, window, hood, or trunk must not have been opened in order to permit the canine to enter. At the traffic stop, if the driver has his window down when the officer approaches the car, then search the car as you have found it with the window down. If the officer finds the window up when he or she comes upon the driver, then the window may not be intentionally opened for the purpose of allowing the dog to enter into or stick its nose into or through the open window.

In *United States v. Stone,* 866 F.2d 359 (10th Cir. 1989), the police stopped a vehicle for speeding on the interstate in New Mexico. During the traffic stop, the officer asked the driver to show him a citation that he (the driver) claimed he had received earlier in the day. The driver, Mr. Stone, got out of his car and opened the hatchback to retrieve the ticket. During the course of the traffic stop, other police officers began to show up on scene and one had a drug detection canine as his partner. The vehicle was presented to the dog in a circular manner. The dog showed some interest underneath the rear area of the automobile. The canine then jumped through the hatchback that was left open by the driver when retrieving his previous citation. The dog located a duffel bag containing methaqualone tablets. The court first considered the issue of the open hatchback. The court held that the defendant voluntarily opened the hatchback and left it open. It also found no evidence that the police asked Mr. Stone to open the hatchback so the dog could jump inside. Therefore, the canine handler searched the automobile with the open hatchback as he found it upon his arrival.

No handler encouragement

The second factor in play for the court's review is the police officer's actions and his or her interaction with the dog during the deployment. Every handler knows that when presenting a vehicle to a dog for an exterior sniff, one must not block the dog's search path to avoid any issues related to cuing the dog. Along the same lines, the officers should not do anything that could be interpreted as inducing the dog to jump into the car. In *United States v. Hutchinson,* 471 F. Supp. 2d 497(M.D. Pa. 2007), the court found that, "Although Officer Carrera's canine entered the interior of the vehicle, it did so on its own initiative after becoming attracted by the odor of narcotics emanating from the car, and found no evidence suggesting that Officer Carrera assisted, facilitated, or otherwise encouraged Zeus's (the dog's) entry into the car's interior."

As a handler under this legal theory, one cannot entice their dog by word or act to enter the vehicle. The officer should not encourage their dog to jump into the car, but merely let the dog go where its nose takes it. The dog must be acting on instinct to find source odor. Any actions, by word or deed, on the part of the handler that might facilitate the leap would be deemed a violation of the Fourth Amendment's protections against unreasonable search and seizure. When a dog is performing an exterior sniff of an automobile and the dog happens to leap into the vehicle while demonstrating signs that it is "in odor," but it has not given a final alert or trained final response before jumping, the officer must not play any role in the dog's instinctive decision to jump into the car or stick its nose in or through the open window in order to pinpoint the source of the odor.

Change in behavior
The last major fact for a judge to consider is whether the dog was in the scent cone or "in odor." Those initial changes of behavior indicate that the dog had shown interest in an area of the car but had not displayed what the handler would call a final alert. Such indicators allow the canine officer to establish that the dog's actions were consistent with what the officer has seen in the past when his dog originally detects narcotics odor. These preliminary actions by the canine allow the handler to testify to the court that the dog was merely doing what it has been trained to do. If he does not observe the first signs of the dog's

Chapter 16: Dogs Jumping Into Cars

■ An officer may not open a vehicle door to allow a K9 to enter, but if a vehicle's door or window is voluntarily opened by the occupants, the dog may enter spontaneously.

change in behavior, the handler is left with only the deployment of his dog and the leap into the car. That standing alone would not be enough to carry the day in court.

Search the car as you find it

As we have discussed previously in this chapter, the emphasis is on *searching the car as you find it.* Do not order the driver to roll down windows or leave doors open. Such actions by you could be argued in court as providing an advantage to the dog by allowing greater access to the odor. If the window is down when you first encounter the driver, and if you order him out of the car and he leaves the window down of his own volition, that's fine, but never order the driver to alter the car's condition. Instead, merely search the car as you find it or as the driver leaves it upon his or her exiting the vehicle. That will avoid legal issue in court. If the window was voluntarily left down, you could choose to roll the window up. That action could never be seen as creating an advantage for your dog: it could only be perceived as providing less access to odor and, therefore, only a disadvantage for the handler and narcotics dog.

Additional federal and state cases

Another federal case dealing with this issue is *United States v. Lyons,* 486 F.3d 367 (8th Cir. 2007). The *Lyons* court held that the canine search of the vehicle was not rendered illegal under the Fourth Amendment by the fact that the vehicle's windows were open, creating the opportunity for the canine to breach the interior of the vehicle. The passenger opened the passenger window without any order or request from the trooper. Nor did the trooper order that the windows remain open. The trooper did nothing to direct or encourage the canine to stick his head through the window.

The federal court system is not the only court system to tackle this issue. The State of Missouri in *State v. Logan,* 914 S.W. 2d. 806 (Mo. App. 1995); the State of Georgia in *Noble v. State,* 640 S.E. 2d 666 (Ga. App. 2006); the State of Maryland in *Cruz v. State,* 895 A.2d 1076 (Md. App. 2006); and the State of Arkansas in *Omar v. State,* 262 S.W. 3d195 (Ark. App. Sept. 2007) have all ruled in a similar fashion as the Federal cases cited previously.

A handler must train on a regular basis, which will enable him to know his dog. Knowing how the dog will react in a variety of deployment scenarios will allow the prepared handler to testify in court as to why his dog did what it did. The dog trying to please "Mom" or "Dad" by leaping into the car to find the source of the narcotics odor in order to win the game is every handler's goal for his canine partner. After all, the dog is just following its instinct when it comes to finding the odor of drugs. One could say it is just a leap of faith.

■ ■ ■

Chapter 17

Money Forfeiture and Contamination Theory

FEDERAL LAW AND MOST STATE LAWS provide for the civil forfeiture of property that is used in connection with the violation of drug laws. When authorities come into lawful contact with someone carrying an unusually large amount of money, the issue of forfeiture can be an open-and-shut case when narcotics also are found at the scene.

In most jurisdictions, any seized property will be forfeited if the government can initially show that a relationship exists between the property and the illegal activity. This requisite relationship varies, however, by jurisdiction. For example, both Florida and Illinois require a showing of probable cause — based on the totality of the circumstances — that a nexus exists between the seized money and the illegal activity. See *People v. $1,124.905 U.S. Currency and One 1988 Chevrolet Astrovan,* 177 N.E.2d 1370 (1997) and *State Dept. of Hway Safety and Motor Vehicles v. Holguin,* 909 So.2d 956 (3rd DCA, 2005), respectively.

Probable cause in the context of civil forfeiture is not as strict as probable cause required to prove criminal conduct. At the federal level, the courts also look at the totality of the circumstances when examining forfeiture issues. However, the circuit courts are split as to whether a nexus or substantial connection is necessary. The choice of standard is important because a substantial connection carries a higher burden than a mere nexus. Nonetheless, the connection must be proven by a preponderance of the evidence. See *U.S. v. Funds in the Amount of Thirty Thousand Six Hundred Seventy Dollars,* 403 F.3d 448 (7th Cir. 2005). *Preponderance of the evidence* means that, more likely than not, the evidence indicates that the money is subject to forfeiture.

It is important to note that the burden of proof is not met merely because the currency has been found in the presence of illegal drugs. Obviously, the presence of illegal narcotics makes it easier for the government to prove its case. However, in many instances, no narcotics are found in conjunction with the currency. This means that authorities must rely on other evidence to meet their burden of proof to convince the courts that the money is indeed "dirty." In other words, what if the government's position largely is based on a positive alert to the money by a trained narcotics dog? Should any weight be given to the dog's reaction in civil forfeiture proceedings?

This chapter discusses the tests or methods the courts use to answer those questions. It focuses on the various types of evidence that can warrant forfeiture when the actual presence of drugs is not a determining factor.

Forfeiture scenarios

A typical scenario would go as follows: authorities come into (hopefully) lawful contact with the claimant. A subsequent search of the claimant's person or vehicle reveals a large amount of money. The money is secured by rubber bands. It is bundled in denominations: a manner usually consistent with drug dealing.

Upon questioning, the claimant is not able to dispel the officer's suspicions of drug activity. Interestingly enough, the claimant may exercise his Fifth Amendment right to remain silent, but not always without consequence. Forfeiture being a civil matter, the election to "plead the Fifth" may still lead to negative assumptions. Officers seize the money and subject it to a narcotics-trained dog sniff. The dog alerts to the cash, but no drug is ever actually found near or on the money.

The government or the Department of Motor Vehicles files a complaint for probable cause and requests an order of forfeiture. The burden is on the government to show that the money should be forfeited. Then it shifts to anyone claiming interest in the money to rebut the government's case or assert a legal defense. This means that, in

Chapter 17: Money Forfeiture and Contamination Theory

some jurisdictions, the defendant will have to demonstrate that he or she was in lawful possession of the money and establish through tax returns or other documentation that the cash is legitimate.

Usually, forfeiture statutes will provide for an "innocent owner" defense. Under that defense, the actual owner of the money may claim that he was unaware that the money was being used in connection with drug activity. That defense will work only if the owner did not have reason to believe so. Ultimately, the court will look at the totality of the circumstances to determine whether probable cause exists. In other words, even though one factor alone may not suffice, all the factors put together may be enough. The court may consider all types of evidence, whether direct or circumstantial. It also may take into account the claimant's prior criminal record, including drug offenses. Even hearsay testimony is allowed.

Take the federal case of *U.S. v. Funds in the Amount of Thirty Thousand Six Hundred Seventy Dollars,* mentioned earlier. In that case, federal agents made lawful contact with a certain Antonio Calhoun at the airport. Calhoun was traveling to Phoenix on a one-way ticket paid for in cash. It was not Calhoun's first cash trip to Phoenix in the past two months. Calhoun's sole luggage was a gym bag that he carried with him.

Apparently, DEA agents had been tipped that an individual resembling Calhoun would be traveling on that day and carrying a lot of cash. Calhoun agreed to speak to the agents. He told them that he was currently unemployed but hoping to find work in Phoenix. When he testified at the forfeiture proceedings, Calhoun was evasive regarding the details and purpose of his trip. Most of the information he provided could not be verified.

At the airport, Calhoun denied carrying any narcotics but confessed to having $1,000 on him. He allowed the agents to search both his bag and his person. In the bag, the agents found two separate bundles of cash. Once more the agents asked Calhoun how much money he was carrying. Calhoun answered, "About $1700." The search of Calhoun's person then revealed an additional $28,970 stuffed into a woman's

K9s In the Courtroom

girdle. The money found in Calhoun's possession amounted to more than $30,000.

The cash was separated into 29 bundles of various denominations of $50, $20, and $10 bills. Agents also noticed that Calhoun had become increasingly nervous throughout their search. Believing the money to be related to drug activity, they seized the money and placed it in a plastic bag. The plastic bag was then put in an empty suitcase and placed in a room with other empty suitcases. A drug detection canine was dispatched to the room and alerted to the suitcase containing the money, indicating the presence of narcotics on the money.

The government sought forfeiture of the money pursuant to 21 U.S.C.A §881(a). Federal Statute 21 U.S.C.A §881(a) specifically addresses forfeitures of property to be used in a narcotics transaction. Accordingly, eligible properties include, but are not limited to, currency, vehicles, aircrafts, drugs, drug paraphernalia, and firearms.

The court ruled in favor of the government. It said that the totality of

■ In many cases, no narcotics are found in conjunction with suspected currency, and authorities must rely on other evidence to meet their burden of proof.

Chapter 17: Money Forfeiture and Contamination Theory

the circumstances clearly indicated a strong relationship between the currency found on Calhoun and illegal drug activity. The factors that came into play were:

1. Calhoun was traveling with just one duffle bag and had no checked luggage;
2. He bought a one-way ticket for which he paid cash;
3. Calhoun lied to the agents regarding the amount of money he was carrying;
4. The unusual amount of money found on Calhoun when he was supposed to be unemployed;
5. The interesting manner in which he carried such a large amount of money;
6. The money was separated into various bundles and denominations;
7. Calhoun's increasing nervousness while talking to the agents;
8. His evasive answers to questioning; and, most interestingly,
9. A positive dog sniff to the money, even though agents found no narcotics at the scene.

Naturally, Calhoun challenged the forfeiture. He claimed that the positive dog alert was irrelevant and prejudicial. His argument was based on what is known as global contamination theory. *Global contamination theory* provides that a positive alert to money by a trained dog does not prove that the money was connected to a drug exchange. This theory is based on the premise that as much as 96 percent of the currency in general circulation is contaminated with traces of cocaine or other controlled substances. Therefore, the dog sniff carries no probative weight and is irrelevant in forfeiture proceedings.

The majority of states and federal circuits have rejected the theory as a means of excluding a canine alert as evidence. In Calhoun's case, the court allowed the dog alert as probative evidence. It likely was the key factor in the government's case.

Discrediting global contamination theory

If global contamination theory holds true, then why would any court consider the canine alert? Shouldn't the dog's reaction be useless? In

K9s In the Courtroom

2005, the Mississippi State Supreme Court tackled those very questions in *Evans v. City of Aberdeen,* 926 So.2d 181 (Miss. 2006). It refused to adopt the theory and practically discredited it. Relying on scientific studies, the Court explained that the answer lies with methyl benzoate, a byproduct of cocaine. Narcotics dogs are not trained to detect cocaine itself, but rather the smell of methyl benzoate. They will alert only when the levels of methyl benzoate, thus cocaine, are substantial.

Methyl benzoate also is extremely volatile and evaporates quickly. Currency circulating in the general population, although tainted for the most part, will not trigger an alert. A trained narcotics dog will alert only to currency that was recently in contact with significant amounts of cocaine. That being said, the party seeking forfeiture still must lay an adequate foundation that the sniff was reliable. Otherwise, that piece of evidence becomes inadmissible.

Reliability can be established in several ways. There must be testimony that the method used to conduct the sniff was proper. In other words, did officers take the necessary precautions to avoid contaminating the money while handling it? Was a sufficiently complete chain of custody made to establish the trustworthiness of the evidence? Was the testing area or container used to deposit the money free of contamination?

In *Aberdeen,* even though the Court rejected the theory, it did not allow the positive alert as evidence on grounds of improper testing methods. The officer who conducted the dog sniff testified that he placed the seized money in a brown paper bag he found in the police station's basement. He could not state with any degree of certainty that the bag or basement was "clean." Additionally, he did not know whether the dog had alerted to the bag itself or the money in the bag.

The dog's trustworthiness is just as important in proving reliability. Usually, the dog's handler will testify to the dog's training in the field. Factors considered include: the date the dog was certified, the types of narcotics it has been trained to detect, the amount of training hours that were involved, and any ongoing recertification. The dog's record of accuracy in detecting narcotics on currency also should be provided.

Chapter 17: Money Forfeiture and Contamination Theory

Cases such as *Aberdeen* clearly indicate that global contamination theory is on the decline. Empirical studies continue to weaken the theory. It may be only a matter of time until it becomes completely obsolete. Should that happen, an increase in forfeited funds due to drug activity undoubtedly will occur. Until then, the party seeking forfeiture will have to rely on other persuasive evidence in the hope that it will meet the legal standard in the particular jurisdiction.

■ ■ ■

Chapter 18

Checking Parcels for Home Delivery

AS THE OLD SAYING GOES, "Neither snow nor rain nor heat nor gloom of night..." prevents the delivery of packages from going forward. One of the most popular methods of transporting narcotics from coast to coast is the private parcel service. UPS, FedEx, and USPS all perform overnight, next-day-air deliveries for a fairly reasonable price. When a supplier's drugs absolutely positively have to be there overnight, those companies provide a service that facilitates the supply and demand of our capitalistic society. They ship millions of packages daily. They cannot inspect them all. This chapter explores and explains the Fourth Amendment issues surrounding parcel inspection. Hopefully, it will motivate handlers by showing that when it is raining, sleeting, hailing, or snowing, they can take their canine partners to the warm, dry confines of the parcel distribution center and sniff packages for dope.

State court rulings

In Florida, the case *Lindo v. State*, 983 So.2d 672 (4th D.C.A. June 2008) was based upon the following facts. An Orlando deputy contacted a local U.S. Border Patrol Agent concerning two packages alleged to contain narcotics that had been shipped to South Florida. The deputy provided the tracking numbers, the origin and destination, and the names of the sender and recipient. The agent did not know, but assumed, that the source of the information was a confidential informant. The agent then conveyed the information to a fellow agent who was a canine handler.

Early the next morning, the canine handler and another agent went

Chapter 18: Checking Parcels for Home Delivery

■ When using your K9 to sniff packages at a distribution center, be sure that any packages of interest are set among four or five other packages to avoid cuing the dog.

to the UPS facility, met with the security manager and, with the tracking numbers provided by the Orlando deputy, retrieved the packages from a delivery truck parked at the loading dock. They set the packages out in a lineup with others and deployed the canine. The dog alerted to the two suspect packages.

The agent contacted a detective of the Miramar/South Broward Task Force, who accepted the packages for a warrant-controlled delivery. Two Miramar detectives obtained a search warrant. They then opened the cardboard boxes and inside each one found a plastic bin containing a bale of marijuana wrapped in plastic. The detectives took a sample of the marijuana, tested it, and repacked the boxes. The detectives obtained a search warrant for the residence, which authorized them to attempt delivery and, once the packages were delivered to someone in the house, enter the residence.

The detectives executed the warrant the next day. The task force set up surveillance and observed two men, one of whom was the defendant, exit the house and leave the premises in separate cars. The two men later returned, but left again in separate cars. One of the detectives, dressed as a UPS delivery person, delivered the packages to the front porch of the house. The defendant returned to the house, parked in the driveway, and took the packages inside. After a while, the defendant left the house again, drove around the neighborhood, and returned. When the defendant exited the house yet again, the detectives followed him in a marked car and executed a traffic stop, because they were unsure whether he had placed the packages in the car.

Law enforcement used the defendant's house key to gain entrance to the residence. They found the opened packages in the middle of a bedroom floor with the marijuana exposed. The packages were identified as the ones that were retrieved from UPS and delivered to the house. The detective read the defendant the entire warrant and Miranda warnings from a prepared card. The defendant agreed to talk to the detective, and told her that he was being paid to accept the packages for another person, whose last name he did not know. The packages were to have arrived the day before, but when they did not come on time, he thought they might have been intercepted.

The State charged the defendant with one count of trafficking in cannabis in an amount in excess of 25 but less than 2,000 pounds. The defendant moved to suppress the evidence. At the suppression hearing, the defendant argued that the State lacked probable cause to seize the packages from UPS because there was no veracity attached to the anonymous tip in Orlando. The State responded that the source of the original tip was irrelevant because law enforcement could have done a random dog sniff at the UPS facility without the tip. Further, the State argued that a brief detention of a container for a dog sniff does not constitute a search and seizure.

In *Lindo,* the District Court of Appeals held that the temporary detention of two packages at a mailing facility was not so unreasonable as to interfere, in any meaningful way, with the defendant's packages and, therefore, the temporary detention was not a "seizure" within the meaning of the Fourth Amendment. Because there was no seizure,

Chapter 18: Checking Parcels for Home Delivery

there was no need for the State to establish reasonable suspicion and, considering that the dog sniff of the packages also was not a search, the defendant's Fourth Amendment rights had not been violated.

Federal court rulings

Along with the Florida case just mentioned, the federal courts have held similar opinions. A recent federal opinion, *U.S. v. Quoc Viet Hoang,* 486 F.3d 1156 (9th Cir. 2007), was based on the following factual scenario. An Orange County, California, Sheriff's Department investigator was inspecting packages at the FedEx World Service Center Office at John Wayne Airport. FedEx Corporate Security had authorized Officer Todd, accompanied by his narcotics detection canine, Otto, to be on its premises. At approximately 9:05 a.m., a FedEx employee allowed the investigator into the facility's hold room. The hold room is used to process parcels as they enter the facility or are sent out for delivery.

At 9:10 a.m., Otto was let into the hold room off lead, where he randomly sniffed approximately seven packages located in various parts of the room. Otto alerted to one of the packages, indicating that he had detected the odor of a controlled substance. Officer Todd examined the package, which was addressed to Hoang at an address in Hawaii, and noticed several features that, based on his experience, suggested that the package contained narcotics.

First, the package was scheduled for priority overnight delivery, and the delivery fee had been paid in cash. Second, no telephone numbers for the sender or recipient were listed on the package. Third, the parcel emanated an odor of coffee, a common masking agent. At 9:15 a.m., Officer Todd confiscated the suspicious package and left his business card with the FedEx employee who had provided access to the hold room. He then locked the package in his airport office and attempted to locate the sender's address. He determined that the sender's address on the package was fictitious. Based on an affidavit containing those facts, an Orange County magistrate judge issued a search warrant for the package at 11:40 a.m. that same day.

The package did contain narcotics. The Orange County Sheriff's

K9s In the Courtroom

Department sent the package to drug-enforcement authorities in Hawaii. They obtained a search warrant. An undercover officer in the guise of a FedEx driver made a controlled delivery of the package to Hoang. Hoang accepted and opened the package. He then unpacked the pseudo-drugs that had been substituted for the methamphetamine. He was subsequently arrested and indicted.

The 9th Circuit held that the 10-minute detention, without reasonable suspicion or probable cause, of an in-transit package addressed to the defendant and located in a parcel delivery company's hold room, which elapsed between the police officer's approved initial entry into the hold room and the officer's ultimate seizure of the package addressed

■ The courts have ruled in numerous cases that a dog sniff of a package at a distribution center does not constitute a search or seizure, nor violate the package owner's Fourth Amendment rights.

Chapter 18: Checking Parcels for Home Delivery

to the defendant after a narcotics canine alerted to methamphetamines, did not constitute a seizure. Therefore, it did not violate the defendant's Fourth Amendment rights regarding any possessory interest in the package, where the delay did not interfere with company's ability to deliver his package on time the next day.

The basic premise of law on the issue of sniffing UPS, FedEx, or USPS overnight packages at the distribution center is that even if the defendant has a reasonable expectation of privacy (which the courts say one does not have) in an in-transit package, no Fourth Amendment violation occurs as result of an initial detention and dog sniff of the package, because neither is a search or seizure. Brief removal of the package from the normal delivery stream does not constitute a seizure because there is no meaningful interference with an individual's possessory interests in that parcel.

The two cases reviewed in this chapter illustrate the legal premise that sniffing packages for narcotics odor is not a search, nor is the temporary possession of the box off the conveyor belt for the purpose of sniffing a seizure. Each handler should be careful to follow the protocol of putting other boxes out with the target box. It's also important to proof items commonly associated with parcels, such as cardboard boxes, plastic, labels, the glue for the edge flaps of the box, and label adhesive. A good solid methodology of systematically following the same search pattern and process related to parcel interdiction will enable you to fend off any defense attorney's attack in court.

So if it is a slow, rainy, snowy, or gloomy day and a handler wants to find a productive, proactive way to use a canine partner, make friends with your local delivery company and sniff some packages. Drug dealers need to be caught before their overnight packages get delivered, and giving the dog handler access to the package-distribution building to catch drug dealers is the least that FedEx or UPS can do for law enforcement.

■ ■ ■

Chapter 19

Warehouses, Storage Units and Commercial Property

THE MORE SUCCESSFUL LAW ENFORCEMENT becomes at catching drug traffickers, the more inventive drug traffickers become at hiding their narcotics. The grow-house/stash-house is becoming more prevalent every day, but its use has a tremendous downside for criminals. Many drug traffickers are no longer willing to risk losing their house under state and federal forfeiture laws. Instead, they have turned to alternative locations, one of the most common of which is the U Store It–style warehouse. Using a commercial storage facility affords drug traffickers a false sense of security because it takes the loss of their home out of the equation and allows them the opportunity to rent a storage unit under a fake identity. This chapter covers the search-and-seizure issues related to a narcotics canine deployment on a warehouse storage unit and a commercial garage, in the hope that it helps law enforcement stay one step ahead of the drug trafficker and his defense attorney.

Warehouse or storage unit

The benchmark of Fourth Amendment analysis has been whether a defendant has a constitutionally protected reasonable expectation of privacy in the place being searched. In *State v. Washburn,* 685 S.E. 2d 555 (N.C.App. 2009), the defendant sought to suppress evidence seized from a search of a rented storage unit.

The evidence at the suppression hearing tended to show that on 18 September 2006, Sergeant R.K. Smith of the Kernersville Police Department received a tip from an informant who had been providing accurate information to him for 13 years. The informant told Sergeant

Chapter 19: Warehouses, Storage Units and Commercial Property

Smith that the defendant kept a large quantity of drugs in a blue toolbox in his garage and rented a climate-controlled storage unit somewhere within the Kernersville town limits. In addition, the informant told Sergeant Smith the defendant's name and address, the model and color of the defendant's truck, and the defendant's license plate number. Sergeant Smith relayed that information to the Kernersville Police Department's Vice and Narcotics Unit. Officer A.B. Cox, a detective with the unit, received the information and contacted Sergeant Smith for more details.

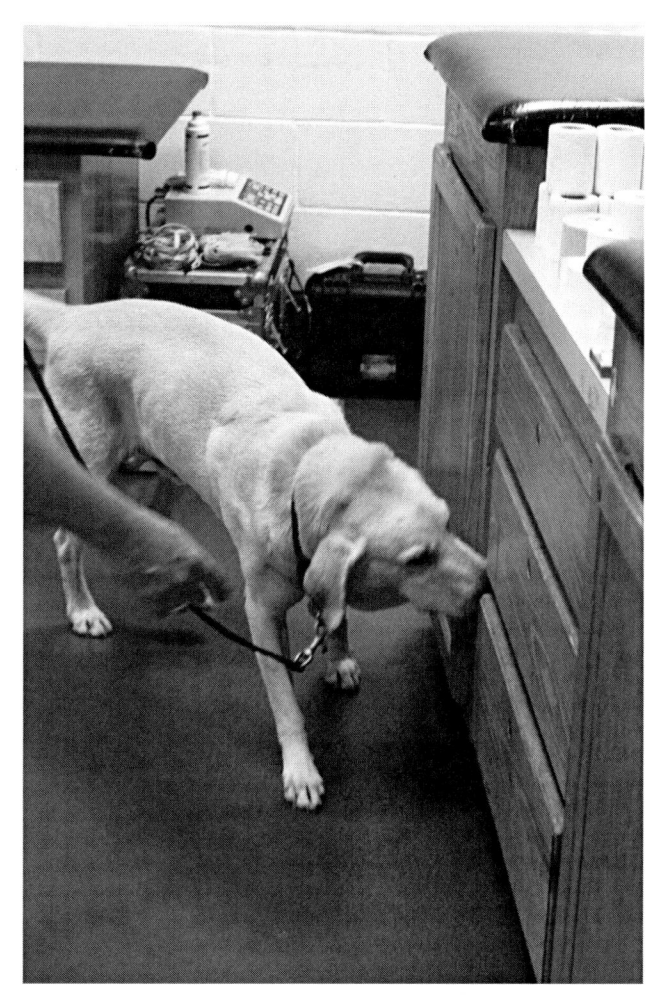

■ Commercial buildings are subject to the ordinary rule that dog sniffs do not expose legitimately private information because they reveal only the presence or absence of odors of contraband.

K9s In the Courtroom

Based on the the tip, Officer Cox began investigating the defendant's activities, conducting surveillance several times at the address supplied by the informant, and visiting Shields Road Self-Storage, the only climate-controlled storage facility in town at that time. Officer Cox confirmed that the defendant lived at the address supplied by the informant after finding mail addressed to the defendant in garbage that was set out for collection. Officer Cox also corroborated the informant's information regarding the defendant's truck, the presence of a blue toolbox in the defendant's garage, and defendant's rental of a storage unit at the storage facility.

To further the investigation, Officer Cox requested that Detective Kevin Clodfelter, a K9 handler, perform a random sweep of the storage facility using his drug detection dog. After he received permission from the manager of the storage facility to enter and search with his K9 partner, Detective Clodfelter began the search. Detective Clodfelter was not provided any information about the specific unit at issue. Once inside the common hallway of the building, the dog indicated the presence of contraband by alerting on the door of unit 4078-C, the defendant's unit. Detective Clodfelter left to obtain a search warrant for the unit. Upon his return with the warrant, the lock to the defendant's unit was drilled off. Inside the unit, the officers discovered drug paraphernalia, a residue of white powder on the floor, and $5,100 in $100 bills.

Based on the evidence seized from the storage unit and the information provided by the informant, police obtained a second search warrant — this one for the defendant's residence. Having knocked on the defendant's door and received no response, the officers entered the residence and found the defendant hiding in the attic. The officers then searched the defendant's home in accordance with the second search warrant.

The defendant's sole argument was that the trial court erred in denying his motion to suppress evidence obtained from both searches conducted by the police department. The defendant contended that the dog sniff of the common hallway outside his locked storage unit constituted an illegal warrantless search, because he had a reasonable

Chapter 19: Warehouses, Storage Units and Commercial Property

expectation of privacy in the storage facility along with the common hallway area. The North Carolina Court of Appeals in *Washburn* disagreed. The Court held that the officers' use of the dog to sweep the common area of a storage facility, alerting them to the presence of contraband in the defendant's storage unit, did not infringe upon the defendant's Fourth Amendment rights. As the defendant had no legitimate interest in possessing contraband, there was no compromise of a legitimate privacy interest, which the Fourth Amendment seeks to protect.

The police officers were lawfully present in the common hallway outside the defendant's individual storage unit. The storage facility consists of several buildings divided into four or five sections, with each section containing 15 units. Renters obtain access to the gated facility by using a personalized access code. The doors to the individual units line the hallways inside the various buildings, and the individual units are secured by the individual renters' locks. The hallway at issue, as with all of the common areas in the facility, was open to every person who had an access code and any invited guests of the renters. The police department also had its own access code supplied by a person with common authority over the building: the facility manager. On the particular day at issue, the police obtained additional permission from the facility manager to access the common areas with a drug dog. The Federal Courts have held in a similar fashion in *U.S. v. Venema,* 563 F.2d 1003 (10th Cir. 1977), and *U.S. v. Brock,* 417 F.3d 692 (7th Cir. 2005).

Some public storage facilities are built with gaps in the roofs of their common ceilings. These gaps could allow for the airflow to travel from unit to unit, just as the wind may affect an open-field sniff, or air conditioning may affect a sniff in a commercial building. A handler must be aware of the structural composition of his surroundings, as the dog's alert to source may be affected by airflow between the units.

In this case, the key factors that allowed the K9 officer to use his dog on the defendant's storage unit were: (1) permission from the warehouse manager to use the dog on the property; (2) the K9 sniff was conducted with the target storage unit unknown to the handler; (3) every storage unit door in the building was presented to the dog in order to isolate and pinpoint the source of any odor detected, excluding all other units; and (4) the sniff was performed from the common hallway for public access, in which all other renters or their guests were free to walk. Using those factors as a guideline for how to conduct a permissible K9 sniff of a rented public storage unit will allow the police K9 handler to be prepared to defend his actions and those of his well-trained and certified narcotics partner in court.

Commercial property

In the recent case of *U.S. v. Parrilla,* U. S. Dist. Ct., S.D. New York, 2014 WL 2111680 (May 13, 2014), the United States District Court for the Southern District of New York declined to extend the philosophy of curtilage of a private home to a commercial business or commercial garage. Simply put, the court did not find that the ruling in *Jardines* applied to commercial property. Therefore, sniffing the door of commercial property (according to this court) is currently still legal even after *Jardines.*

It is true that the Fourth Amendment protects as "houses" places such as garages, business offices, stores, and warehouses, and prohibits warrantless physical entries into such places. And as Justice Scalia recognized in *Jardines,* the Fourth Amendment also considers curtilage "the area 'immediately surrounding and associated with the home,' " to be "part of the home itself for Fourth Amendment purposes." (133 S.Ct. at 1414.) As a result, the dog sniff on *Jardines's* front porch took place in a constitutionally protected area because the porch was considered part of his home.

However, the area surrounding a business has never been considered part of the business itself, and the concept of curtilage is limited to the home. Neither the Supreme Court nor the Second Circuit has adopted the notion of "business curtilage" advanced by the defendant. Moreover, while a few courts have held investigations of exterior areas surrounding a business to be "searches," they have done so exclusively through application of the *Katz* framework.

Chapter 19: Warehouses, Storage Units and Commercial Property

■ A K9 sniff on commercial property is not subject to the same philosophy of curtilage that applies to a residence.

In this case, the defendant Parrilla attempted to convince the Court to make a novel extension of the law. The Fourth Amendment's traditional property rights baseline is not an appropriate vehicle for such an endeavor, as it protects only those rights that are traditionally accepted and specifically enumerated. In *Jardines,* Justice Scalia remarked that, "one virtue of the Fourth Amendment's property-rights baseline is that it keeps easy cases easy." (133 S.Ct. at 1417.) There, the Court had "no doubt" that officers entered a constitutionally protected area, because "the front porch is the classic exemplar of an area adjacent to the home and 'to which the activity of home life extends.' " (Id. at 1415.) Here, the Court has no doubt that officers did not enter a constitutionally protected area, because the unenclosed areas surrounding a business have never been considered part of the inside of such a property for constitutional purposes.

Moreover, not only are reasonable expectations of privacy in commercial premises simply lower than those in a home, commercial premises lacking "the Fourth Amendment sanctity of the home" also are qualitatively different in an important way. Homes are places where "all details are intimate details, because the entire area is held safe from prying government eyes." (See *Kyllo*.) Commercial premises are not private places where all details are intimate and private, and Courts have declined to extend *Kyllo* beyond the home.

Nonresidential commercial places are therefore subject to the ordinary rule that dog sniffs do not expose legitimately private information because they reveal only the presence or absence of the odors of contraband. Because commercial premises are not a place where "all details are intimate details," (see *Kyllo*), a canine sniff that reveals the scent of contraband escaping from within a commercial building does not violate the proprietor's reasonable expectations of privacy. The Court concludes that the canine sniffs at Parrilla's (commercial) garage did not violate his reasonable expectations of privacy and were not searches under the meaning of the Fourth Amendment.

Therefore, the law related to both warehouses/storage units and commercial property/ garages seems to be currently unaffected by the recent ruling by the U.S. Supreme Court's ruling in *Jardines*. (See Chapter 14 on dogs sniffing houses.) The basic rule of thumb for a narcotics dog deployment in this area boils down to two questions: (1) "Am I, the handler, lawfully present with my dog to perform the sniff ?" and (2) "Does the location being sniffed have a constitutionally protected area or reasonable expectations of privacy such as one's home?" If the answers to those questions are respectively (1) "yes" and (2) "no," then the law on dogs sniffing houses would not apply nor restrict the narcotics dog handler from deploying his or her canine.

■ ■ ■

Chapter 20

Legal Issues in Using Gun Dogs

IN THE EVER-EVOLVING WORLD OF POLICE CANINE USE, it has become popular to find additional ways to use the dog's exceptional scent-detection abilities. Police around the world regularly use dogs to locate narcotics and bombs and to track humans. Law enforcement also has branched out by using detection dogs in unique applications such as agriculture, fish and wildlife, and even to detect illegal cell phones in prisons. One of the newest trends gaining acceptance across the country is the use of a well-trained canine partner to detect firearms. This chapter highlights the legal and practical issues in using this valuable resource.

Gun searches and probable cause

It goes without saying that a gun dog is merely an investigative tool used to find or locate items. The plain possession of a firearm, in and of itself, is not illegal as compared with possession of narcotics. Depending on the laws of each state, citizens may legally possess guns in myriad ways. Therefore, deploying a well-trained gun dog will not necessarily provide law enforcement with probable cause to search, because possessing a gun is not, under general circumstances, illegal.

Article searches

The most common use of a gun dog that immediately comes to mind is the article search. For example, an armed robbery suspect is on the loose and, while running from police, is seen to discard an object in a field or over a fence before being taken into custody. A lot of police

K9s In the Courtroom

departments currently have well-trained tracking dogs that can find articles such as guns by locating the human suspect's scent left on the gun handle. However, the human scent on the firearm could be affected by the length of time in the field, the elements the gun was exposed to, and the conditions under which the gun was carried or possessed. One such condition that should be considered is finding a gun that was tossed while a fleeing suspect was wearing gloves. In such a case, the gun will maintain its natural odor longer than it would retain the human scent left on the gun handle during a traditional article search performed by a tracking dog. An advantage of a gun dog is that it is trained to focus on odor that relates exclusively to the oils, powder, and residue commonly associated with a discharged firearm, rather than on human odor.

Another benefit to using a gun canine under the aforementioned set

■ Gun dogs are trained to find the odor of gunpowder and ammunition versus the odor of human scent, which is an advantage if a suspect is wearing gloves or discards a gun when fleeing the scene of a crime.

Chapter 20: Legal Issues in Using Gun Dogs

of circumstances is that the dog handler does not have to worry about human scent contamination of the area to be searched. At some point, every handler has come across a scene where his or her colleagues have inadvertently trampled through the area to be searched. Now, with the use of a gun dog, those issues are no longer a concern for the gun dog handler who is trying to locate a firearm, because the dog focuses only on the odor associated with guns and ammunition.

Using a gun dog when executing a search warrant

Using a drug dog during the execution of a narcotics-search warrant makes good sense. The judge who issued the warrant has found probable cause that drugs would be present at a certain location, and a drug dog's talent to detect and pinpoint drug odor is an invaluable tool in finding drugs in unique hiding places that might ordinarily be overlooked. The dog's nose is a tool that relates to finding the focus of the warrant: drugs. But what about using a gun dog during the execution of a drug-search warrant?

That question can be difficult to answer under certain circumstances. If one has a standard, controlled buy of cocaine and nothing else, the answer would have to be "no." Law enforcement is allowed or authorized by the judge to look only for the items for which probable cause has been proven. In the previous example, the item in question would be cocaine only. How would a gun dog aid you in finding cocaine? It would not. Would you bring a bomb dog to execute your narcotics-search warrant? You would not, because bomb dogs are of no use in finding drugs. The same would be said for a gun dog.

However, what if during the controlled buy of cocaine a confidential informant tells the police that the defendant either had a gun on him or a gun was seen within ready reach of the defendant? Does that change things? A good argument could be made that it does. If being in possession of a firearm during the commission of a felony — such as selling dope out of a house in the previous example — is a crime, as it is in most jurisdictions, then the judge could rightfully authorize the police to look for evidence of commission of that secondary crime. That would be possession of the gun. If the pot is sweetened and the target is a convicted felon, being in or around a gun at the time of the controlled buy is a valid secondary charge. In such a case, the use of a gun dog would be a valuable tool in locating the handgun inside the house during execution of the warrant.

The general use of a gun dog during a basic drug warrant could end in a motion to suppress, with issues as to why the gun dog was used if the warrant contained no evidence of gun use or possession in the house being searched. However, legal philosophy and case law suggest that drugs and guns go together. If you are executing a drug–search warrant on a residence, you may have a valid reason to use a gun dog in the home because a handful of cases recognize the premise that drugs and guns go hand-in-hand. Therefore, where you have probable cause to find drugs, it could be argued that it is likely that an officer would encounter a firearm in or around the same location. So the use of a gun dog during a narcotics–search warrant is not all that far-fetched.

Gang or homicide search warrants

Another helpful area for the practical use of a gun dog is during the execution of a search warrant at an urban location that a violent gang uses as a flophouse. If the police can relate the house to violent gang activity, and relate those gang members living at the residence to some gun history, the police stand a good chance of convincing the judge to allow them to look for weapons relating to a drive-by shooting known to have been committed by the gang. Hopefully, discovering a gun could lead to a ballistic match that could solve the crime.

In the same vein, a gun dog would be useful in searching the house, attic, garage, or yard for the gun hidden in a domestic-style or staged home invasion, robbery, burglary, or homicide. On some occasions, the firearm actually is hidden on the premises. The homicide detectives develop probable cause to search a location for evidence including the possible murder weapon. The gun dog would be an excellent asset to have at the police department's disposal in an attempt to locate the

Chapter 20: Legal Issues in Using Gun Dogs

weapon in a timely manner or direct the detectives to a unique search area that might be overlooked by the human eye.

Also, a well-trained and maintained gun dog has the ability not only to find firearms, but also to find shell casings. At first blush, being called to a scene to find shell casings does not seem to be fruitful to a basic investigation, but technology allows a crime lab to match spent shell casings to each other and eventually to a firearm. If your crime lab can determine that shell casings located at crime scene "A" and, weeks later, shell casings located at crime scene "B" were fired from the same gun, you can now show that your crimes are related. Law enforcement can then explore that relationship to find other commonalities at the crime scenes, or to compare common traits of the victims, all of which could narrow your field of possible suspects.

■ Guns and drugs are often found together, so finding one could lead to finding the other.

Consent searches

Valuable information comes across the desk of law enforcement every day, and sometimes that information relates to finding a murder weapon stored or hidden at a third party's house or apartment. On occasion, information needs to be acted upon quickly without time for a search warrant, or the information obtained by law enforcement does not provide enough detail to establish probable cause for a search warrant. Those circumstances leave police the option of obtaining consent to search the location for the firearm. If consent is obtained, using a gun dog allows police to quickly and efficiently search for gun odor without having to "toss" the place.

Remember, never have the dog present during a request for consent to search. Not having the dog present lessens the coercive appearance of the request, as consent must be freely and voluntarily given. On a consent search, dealing with the suspect's parents or grandparents in an effective and professional manner could make all the difference in finding the gun. A well-trained gun dog can provide law enforcement with such an option.

Probation and parole sweeps

Often, probation or parole officers call upon police to assist them in an administrative search of a defendant's residence. Police officers should check with their local jurisdictions, but most areas of the country do not allow probationers to possess, or even live, in a place where there is access to firearms (even if the firearms belong to a parent or roommate). A gun dog locating a firearm — or even ammunition — could enable law enforcement to pursue a probation or parole violation in court and lead to finding the probationer in violation of his supervision.

School searches

School violence is on the rise. Gun dog and narcotics dog sniffs have become a popular tool in helping school administrators combat such activity. If you are asked to have your dog perform such a sniff, be sure you have permission from the school's principle or other high-ranking school official.

If you have a tip about a particular student and you are going to run lockers for odor, run all the lockers in the row without knowing which locker belongs to the student in question. Running the row of lockers "blind" to the handler will prove advantageous down the road in terms of your dog's reliability, and will prevent any argument that your dog was cued to a particular locker or location.

As the handler, note the area of the alert and notify the school officials, but do not search the area yourself. Remember, you are using

Chapter 20: Legal Issues in Using Gun Dogs

your dog as a tool for an administrative search by school officials to help them pinpoint possible areas of concern. It is not a criminal search or investigation until school personnel find drugs or a gun.

It is plain to see from the various examples discussed that a gun dog could be a new and valuable resource for a large urban police department or for a sheriff's office responsible for a large area of the state. A gun dog can provide an officer with additional options for finding a gun, ammunition, or casings, all of which could lead to solving crimes and holding defendants responsible for their criminal acts.

■ ■ ■

Chapter 21

Basic Testimony 101

CANINE OFFICERS OFTEN TESTIFY in front of judges who have little working knowledge of how an officer performs his duties. Handlers are questioned by lawyers who sometimes know even less than judges do. That is why it is imperative that you dot every "i" and cross every "t" when testifying. Officers should avoid the trap of not being precise in *what* is said or in *how* it is said. This chapter points out eight basic areas that canine officers should focus on in order to be clear and concise in their testimonies before the court.

Odor, not drugs

It is common knowledge that a well-trained police canine will alert to the odor of four or five basic narcotics. However, in courtroom testimony or a deposition, handlers can get lazy. All too often they mistakenly testify that, "My dog alerted to the cocaine," or "My dog alerts to the presence of a narcotic substance." Are those statements true and correct? Better ways to articulate the concept would be: "My dog alerted to the *odor* of one of the four narcotics that it is trained to detect," or "My dog alerted to the presence of the odor of narcotics being present." The point is to emphasize that odor is truly what the dog is trained to detect, and odor is truly what the dog finds or alerts on.

One should not convey the false impression that dogs find drugs, because they don't. Dogs alert to odor, direct the handler to the source of the odor, and then the officer searches for drugs in the area where source odor was indicated. Every handler has had an alert to a vehicle in which odor was present but no drugs were found. That does not

Chapter 21: Basic Testimony 101

shock the canine handler when it happens, and it should not shock the judge or the lawyers involved in the case once they learn that a dog does not find drugs but, instead, merely alerts to the drug's odor.

Sniff, search, or scan

Has your dog ever been deployed to search a vehicle? Searching, under the law, embraces a defendant's protected rights. Searching invokes the United States Constitution and all its various personal protections from illegal government action. You don't want to use the term *search,* because lawyers and judges are trained in law school that a search must be *reasonable* under the U.S. Constitution. The term *sniff* does not raise such a thought process in lawyers or judges. Therefore, has your dog ever been deployed to sniff the exterior of a vehicle? The point illustrated here is the terminology of *search* versus *sniff.* Always use the term *sniff* when testifying about using and deploying your dog. Remember, it is the exterior sniff and final alert to odor from outside the car that allows the police officer to search the automobile's interior.

Some officers like to use the word *scan.* But scan is a visual term commonly used in relation to sight. The dog is not being used for its unique eyesight, but rather for its unique sense of smell. Therefore, has the dog been deployed to scan a vehicle? No. The canine has been deployed to sniff a vehicle.

Courtroom demonstrations

Don't fall into the trap of being challenged to do either a courtroom demonstration of your canine's ability or to recreate the stop and deployment of your dog on a vehicle or within a house. The courtroom demonstration is a big no-no, because the courtroom is not a controlled environment. Courtrooms are public areas. You have zero control over who was in there 10 minutes ago and what drug or drug odor they had on them. Plus, narcotics odor commonly occurs in a courthouse because drug trials take place in them every day of the week. You cannot control the air conditioning and the airflow. Also, it is not beyond the realm of possibility that a defense attorney will play foul by planting odor in a trashcan in the courtroom and wait for your dog to alert to it. Stay away from courtroom demonstrations, because more harm than good can come out of them.

Never fall for the request to recreate the deployment of your dog from six months ago or, for that matter, from last night. Why? Because, again, you can never recreate the scene with a car and an odor exactly the way it was that night. You will not have the same wind direction, air currents, or temperatures. You may have found a crack rock on the car's floorboard, but your dog alerted to the odor of the marijuana joint the driver finished smoking 20 minutes ago. The point being, as a handler, you can never recreate all the surrounding circumstances that led to the canine's alert on the night of the arrest. Therefore, don't do it.

Dead scent, stale or lingering odor

One of my favorite areas of testimony involves the defense attorney's fictitious terms *dead scent* and *stale odor*. Let's define these oxymoronic terms: *dead,* meaning no longer alive or no longer in existence or use; and *scent*, meaning a distinctive odor. Now let's examine the illogical meaning of the defense attorney's question, "Has your dog ever alerted to a dead scent?" How could a dog alert to a distinctive odor that is no longer in existence? If it is longer in existence then, by definition, the odor is not present and a dog could not alert to it.

Next let's define *stale odor*. Stale means having lost freshness. Does your dog have the ability to discern freshness? No, a dog only has the ability to determine that odor is or is not present. A dog does not alert by lifting its right hind leg for stale odor that's more than 10 hours old or its left hind leg for fresh odor that's less than 10 hours old.

For a dog, and in your testimony, odor is odor. It is either there or it is not there. Do not fall into the trap of legitimizing questions that use those terms by trying to answer them. Instead, explain that such statements truly do not make sense as applied to narcotics dog handling. Do not be afraid to ask the defense attorney what he or she means in using those terms. This is kind of fun, because most of attorneys do not themselves understand the terms, nor can they explain them to you. This

Chapter 21: Basic Testimony 101

■ When defense attorneys toss fictitious terms such as "dead scent" and "stale odor" around, ask them to explain what they mean by those terms.

leaves them with no place to go with their questioning and forces them to move on to another line of questioning.

Lastly, one of my personal favorites is the idea of lingering odor. Will your dog alert to a lingering odor? *Linger* means to remain alive; to continue to persist although gradually dying, ceasing, or disappearing. Will your dog alert to an odor that remains alive or that continues to exist? What about the fact that the narcotics odor maybe be gradually weakening or disappearing? Think about that for a second. What odor does not exist while slowly dissipating or weakening over time until eventually it is gone?

Yes, that cat is out of the proverbial bag K9 handlers; odor will eventually become so weak that it will become nonexistent. Does anyone other than a defense lawyer trying to fool a judge really think that odor will last forever? All odors linger at some point. A handler should never fall into these traps and try to label odor. Odor is odor is odor, folks, and it is either present in sufficient quantities for your dog to detect or it is not. It is just that simple.

K9s In the Courtroom

Train on all odors

Obtaining a narcotics certification for your dog from a recognized canine national organization is preferred. But make sure that the certification includes testing for all odors that your dog is trained to detect. How valuable is a canine certification that merely tests for cocaine and marijuana when the dog also is trained to alert to heroin and methamphetamine?

Along those lines, every handler should train weekly on all odors without exception. When asked to explain your training methods, it's important to emphasize that you vary the amounts of each drug to provide varying amounts of odor. In addition, always remember to use a variety of locations when hiding the drugs in vehicles, rooms, and luggage. Never allow yourself to fall into lazy training habits that will leave you open to criticism from skilled defense attorneys on cross-examination in the courtroom.

False alert

Let's examine a favorite, artful defense attorney term: *false alert*. How many handlers across the country have encountered the question, "Well officer, has your dog ever false-alerted?" Every handler will be asked that question at some point in his or her career. When responding to the question of your dog making a mistake, you need only deal with the idea of false alert as it relates to training sessions or certification, never as it relates to real-world, on-duty deployments. (See Chapter 13 on Dog Reliability)

That difference is of tremendous importance because training is done in a controlled environment, whereas real-world deployments always contain an unknown factor in an alert to odor where no drugs are found. The false-alert question is fair for a handler to answer *only* when it is phrased in terms of a controlled setting. It is impossible to answer in the setting of a real-world deployment. As a handler, never allow a defense attorney to suggest, infer, or get you to admit that an alert to drug odor outside a vehicle within which no drugs were found is a false alert. It is not!

Chapter 21: Basic Testimony 101

Therefore, when asked whether your dog has ever alerted to odor where no actual drugs have been found, answer, "yes." When the attorney says, "Then your dog has falsely alerted, right?" answer "no." Defense attorneys confuse the two scenarios all too often. A handler should not make that mistake.

Canine mistakes

"Has your dog ever made a mistake?" is a common question posed by defense attorneys. The answer to that question could be "yes" or "no." Handlers should answer that question only as it relates to a controlled setting in which drugs are known to be present, such as a certification exam or weekly training. A canine officer should never answer the question if it refers to real-world deployments, because too many unknown factors exist.

Now, if a dog has alerted to the four odors of narcotics and also, unfortunately, to duct tape, would you say that the dog was making a mistake in alerting to the duct tape? The answer is "No." Why? Because if the dog accidentally was trained to find cocaine, heroin, marijuana, methamphetamine, and duct tape, you definitely have a training issue to address. Proofing your dog off of common odors needs to be done in training, which is where the mistake was made to begin with. The dog was only doing what it thought it was trained to do. So, if your dog has come to believe that duct tape is an odor it should alert to, did the dog make a mistake? No, the dog was only finding what it was inadvertently trained to find. The handler should note that issue in training records, fix the issue, always proof off the inadvertent odor in the future, and move on in working the dog.

Proofing

Proofing is an important aspect of training, because your record of it shows that your dog truly alerts only to drug odor. Keep a running list of the items you proof off of during weekly training. Handlers also should keep a running list of real-world deployments and where drugs were found, as well as document the surrounding conditions and items that were present when the drugs were discovered. Common items including cigars, cigarettes, fast-food items, plastic, tape, grease, and air freshener (to name a few) should be documented. Being able to tell a judge that those items are regularly displayed on a monthly basis, and that your canine partner does not show any interest in them in training or in the real world, is key to establishing that your dog is reliable.

Hopefully, those testimonial tips will allow handlers to convey information to a prosecutor or judge in a clear, concise manner, and help deflect some of the common defense attorney tricks of the trade. Work with your prosecutor in advance of your motion or trial. Aid them in understanding how your canine works and what questions are good to ask in court. Work together as a team. Good, solid courtroom testimony from the canine handler is the foundation for successful prosecution in a court of law based upon canine alert.

■ ■ ■

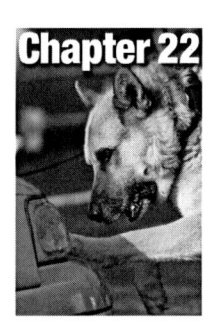

Chapter 22
Courtroom Testimony

NOT ONLY DO YOU HAVE TO KEEP well-documented training and deployment records, you also must be able to explain why the records you keep are valuable and able to prove your dog reliable. In this chapter, we discuss some common questions from defense attorneys and what records you will use to prove your dog reliable in court.

Discrediting testimony

Defense attorneys will attempt to discredit your dog's ability in finding target odor only. They will make the argument that your dog will find not only the illicit target odors, but also many other legal odors. Following are some typical questions asked by defense attorneys.

- "Have you as a handler ever committed a mistake that caused your canine to alert/indicate when no drug odor was present?"
- "Isn't it possible that your dog alerts to the plastic bag?"
- "How do you know that your dog indicated to the odor of the alleged drug and not to some other odor?"
- "Isn't it true that on occasion your dog finds drugs concealed in tobacco? Isn't it also true that you reward your dog for that? Is it possible that your dog has been trained to find tobacco?"
- "Deputy, referring back to this specific case, the drugs my client is charged with posessing were found inside of a tobacco pouch. Can you show me in your training records, or any records, where you can prove your dog was not alerting to tobacco?"

All of those questions focus on the dog learning to indicate to an additional odor other than the illicit target odor. This is where you will need to have training records that specifically denote proofing of items used in the packaging of target odor in training, and also the packaging used on drugs found in real-life deployments. Also, you may need to use any other legal odors that may be commonly found on or around target odor during training. An explanation of extinction training may be necessary to show that you know how to counter-condition the dog to an incorrect odor that was inadvertently trained.

The defense will focus questions on your deployment/use log. They will ask questions related to indications/alerts where no drugs were found, such as

- "Has your dog ever falsely alerted/indicated?"
- "Has your dog ever alerted/indicated to anything other than drug odor?"

The term all defense attorneys and most handlers focus on is *false alert.* Defense attorneys coined that term to imply that the dog has the ability to alert/indicate mistakenly. If you are asked a question using the term *false alert,* ask the attorney to define the term. They likely will answer, "An indication/alert where no target substance is found."

In *Florida v. Harris,* the U.S. Supreme Court has somewhat answered this question for you:

"Making matters worse, the decision below treats records of a dog's field performance as the gold standard in evidence, when in most cases they have relatively limited import. Errors may abound in such records. If a dog on patrol fails to alert to a car containing drugs, the mistake will usually go undetected because the officer will not initiate a search. Field records thus may not capture a dog's false negative. Conversely (and more relevant here), if a dog alerts to a car in which the officer finds no narcotics, the dog may have not made a mistake at all. The dog may have detected substances that were too well hidden or present in quantities too small for the officer to locate. Or the dog may have smelled the residual odor of drugs previously in the vehicle or on the driver's person. Field data thus may markedly overstate a dog's real false positives."

Handlers should not concede the existence or accuracy of the term

Chapter 22: Courtroom Testimony

false alert. A dog's alert/indication is a trained behavior, not a decision the dog makes on its own. For the dog to have a correct and accurate indication/alert to an odor other than a target odor, it must have been trained to find that odor. Which defies the term *false.* If you trained the dog to find an odor other than a target odor, whether intentionally or unintentionally, how could that be false? You trained the dog to do it.

This forces the question back to its appropriate place in training, as explained by the U.S. Supreme Court in *Florida v. Harris:*

"By contrast, those inaccuracies — in either direction — do not taint records of a dog's performance in standard training and certification settings. There, the designers know where drugs are hidden and where they are not — and so where a dog should alert and where he should not. The better measure of a dog's reliability thus comes away from the field, in controlled testing environments."

Handlers should use their training records involving proofing and controlled negatives to show that their dogs are well trained. When correct proofing items are used and documented, records can prove that the dog will indicate/alert *only* to the target odor. Using blanks or controlled negatives also shows that the dog can accurately clear in an environment absent of drug odor by *not* indicating/alerting, thus showing a correct response by the dog.

Another angle the defense will use involves statistics related to deployments. They will argue as follows:
- Fifty vehicles were inspected.
- Ten of the vehicles have alerts/indications.
- Six of the ten vehicles contained drug substance.
- Four of the ten vehicles do not contain drug substance.

The defense will contend that the dog is wrong 40 percent of the time — at best, correct 60 percent of the time.

Handlers should argue that because training focuses on controlled negatives or blank exercises, and these are exercises that do not contain any target odor, the correct action by the dog is no indication at all. Using the numbers above,
- Forty of the fifty total vehicles were inspected and found to not

contain a target odor; this is a correct response proven by training.
- Drug substance was found in the vehicle six times.
- Which brings you to 92 percent correct.

Don't stop there: in the last chapter we discussed verifying your indication. Verification is based on corroborating information that substantiates the dog's alert/indication. If the driver of the vehicle admits to previously possessing a target odor in the vehicle, the indication will be substantiated. If the vehicle recently was involved in a drug transaction, that would substantiate the dog's indication/alert. For the sake of argument, if you had only two of the four indications/alerts where no drugs were found with verifications, that brings you to 96 percent correct. With proper training, every indication or non-indication is a correct response from the dog.

Some defense attorneys will attack the process of training the dog. They will challenge what you know as a handler and how well you can explain what you know to a judge. For example: "Do you train against the possibility of your dog alerting to dead scents/residual odors?" What is a *dead scent* or *residual odor*? Those terms are oxymoron in the detection world. I suppose they refer to odor that is present after the target substance has been removed. But why do we label that odor differently than when substance is present? The odor present in either situation is the same. Odor is odor, whether substance is present or was recently present and has been removed. Handlers should be diligent in explaining that to the judge to be sure they are not confused by a defense term. If a handler would attempt to train the dog to not alert/indicate when odor is present but substance is not, that would cause the dog to be more unreliable than reliable.

Another defense question might be, "How long does odor last?" That question is difficult if not impossible to answer with any certainty. Many factors play a role in the presence of odor: packaging, placement, wind, temperature, humidity, length of time concealed and, to a limited extent, what surface the substance was on or contained in.

"What, specifically, are your goals for training?" That question pushes the handler to have a plan for every training exercise. No team,

Chapter 22: Courtroom Testimony

■ Dogs are trained to find odor, not substance; that is what you will have to explain and defend in a court of law.

professional or otherwise, practices as if it was a full-on game. All teams practice the basics: batting, pitching, catching, and the mental aspects of the game. Canine training should mimic that style of practice. If all of the basic handling essentials are done properly and consistently, when a game is played the outcome should be victorious.

"Does your dog find drugs?" is a common question with an even more common answer: "My dog finds the odor of drugs, not the drug substance itself.

"Does your dog make mistakes?" That is question that you must evaluate from the dog's perspective. A mistake is something that a person makes when choosing an answer to a question. It involves rational thought that the dog cannot do. The dog responds to a conditioned stimulus — it does not evaluate the decision. If the dog did make mistakes, and the entire decision process was in the dog's mind, and the reaction from the dog was exactly the same if odor was present and was not present, how could we as handlers ever say whether the dog was reacting to odor or not? How could we correct any behavior? How could the dog ever be considered reliable?

"Has your dog ever missed finding drugs?" If your dog is properly conditioned, the dog will react the same every time it encounters a trained odor. Substance can be present and, due to many factors, the dog is never in the area where odor is present. Or no odor is escaping from the target substance. If the dog does not smell the odor, it will not react.

"How does your dog indicate to drug odor?" Your dog has a consistent and demonstrative reaction when the odor of a target substance is detected. That reaction is commonly called the *behavior change*. Shortly after the behavior change, your dog will trace the odor to source and display the final response, which typically is a "sit," "scratch," or "bite" at the source of the odor. Explain the entire response, not just the final response.

"Have you ever cued your dog?" Some defense experts and scientists call inadvertent cuing the "Clever Hans" effect. Those of us who have been teaching handlers to prevent that effect for the past 20 years have called it *cuing*. No matter what it's called, it can and will affect your reliability. It's up to you to perfect your handling skills to eliminate this effect from your performance.

The history of Clever Hans

During the early twentieth century, the public was especially interested in animal intelligence due in large part to Charles Darwin's publications. Hans was a horse owned by Wilhelm von Osten, who was a mathematics teacher, an amateur horse trainer, and something of a mystic. Von Osten claimed that Hans had been taught to add, subtract, multiply, divide, and work with fractions; tell time; keep track of the calendar; differentiate musical tones; and read, spell, and understand German. Von Osten would ask questions and Hans would answer by tapping his hoof. Questions could be asked both orally and in written form.

Due to public interest, the German Board of Education formed a commission to investigate von Osten and Hans. The commission

Chapter 22: Courtroom Testimony

consisted of a veterinarian, a circus manager, a cavalry officer, a number of schoolteachers, and the director of the Berlin Zoological Gardens. The commission deemed that no tricks were involved in Hans' and von Osten's performance. They passed the investigation off to Oskar Pfungst, a German comparative biologist and psychologist who tested the claimed abilities by
- isolating Hans (horse) from von Osten (handler),
- isolating both Hans and von Osten from the spectators,
- using someone other than von Osten to ask the questions, and
- varying whether the questioner knew the answer to the question they were asking Hans.

Pfungst ruled out fraud in his investigation, noting that no matter who asked the question, Hans still provided the correct answer. However, Pfungst noticed that Hans only provided the correct answer when his questioner or the audience knew the correct answer themselves. In this environment, Hans provided the correct answer 89 percent of the time. When Hans could not see the questioner or audience, or if neither of them knew the answer, Hans only provided the correct answer 6 percent of the time.

Pfungst concluded that Hans was, in fact, recognizing and reacting to minute, unintentional facial and postural changes in both the questioner and audience. Pfungst noticed that when Hans would approach the correct number of taps, tension would grow in von Osten. When Hans reached the proper number of taps, that tension would be released. The *Clever Hans Effect* has become a widely accepted example of not only the involuntary cues provided by onlookers in possession of knowledge that others do not possess, but also animals' ability to notice and react to subtle cues provided by others around them.

Cuing test

How does the case of Clever Hans apply to you? Defense experts are using the information from the 1904 investigation by Pfungst, along with a 2010 study by Lisa Lit, a postdoctoral fellow at the University of

K9s In the Courtroom

California Davis Department of Neurology. Lit enlisted 18 drug and bomb detection handlers and canines to participate in this study. The study was designed to determine whether, if the handlers were told and believed that drugs or bomb materials were present in an environment, they would exhibit cues or behaviors that the dog would read and react to.

Handlers were told verbally and in writing that there were four inspection areas, two of which contained an odor their dogs were trained to detect, and the locations of these odors were marked with a red piece of paper. The remaining two inspection areas contained distracter odors such as food and toys. In reality, the handlers were lied to and none of the areas contained an odor their dogs were trained to detect.

The area used for this study was a church that Lit was confident had never contained drug or bomb odor in the past. Inspection area #1 contained no odor placed by the study group and no red paper markers. It was a room essentially as they found it in the church. Inspection area #2 contained the red pieces of paper. The handlers were told and believed that the red pieces of paper marked the location where the target odors were concealed. Inspection area #3 contained food and toys concealed in unmarked locations. Inspection area #4 contained food and toys that were marked with red pieces of paper. The handlers were told that these red pieces of paper marked the locations of the odors that their dogs were trained to find.

The hoax was well acted out by the study group. The target odors they were hiding were shown to the handlers and carried into the rooms. The metal containers the target odors were contained in reportedly were placed on the ground near the door and not taken any further into the room. Reportedly, the odors were inside three layers of plastic bags and the metal containers were never opened.

The teams inspected each area twice for a total of eight deployments. Those eight deployments generated 225 incorrect indications/alerts. Every indication/alert called by the teams was incorrect: no target odors were actually concealed in the inspection areas. The study

Chapter 22: Courtroom Testimony

cites two possible reasons for the incorrect alerts: 1. handlers were erroneously calling alerts on locations they believed contained target scent or, 2. the handlers' knowledge or belief that odor was present in the rooms affected the behavior of their dogs. Dogs were alerting to the handlers' behavior and not a target odor, as in the Clever Hans Effect.

The author admits that telling the handlers that a target odor existed at the red paper markers could have influenced the handlers' interpretation of the canines' behavior, but it does not explain the numerous other alerts/indications called by the handlers at locations that did not have a red paper marker. Post-test interviews of the handlers revealed three of the handlers admitted to overtly cuing their dogs to respond to the locations of the red paper markers. The author discarded this information, citing the fact that all observers were familiar with detection dog training and performance. All observers were visibly surprised to hear the three handlers' admissions. In Lit's opinion, it is unlikely, but admittedly cannot be confirmed, that handlers called alerts on markers without seeing an appropriate behavior from the dog.

Lit is aware of other reasons that could cause incorrect responses. The first possibility is that the area was previously contaminated with target odor: Lit feels that reason is unlikely due to the large number of alerts to marked sites as well as the array of alert locations. Also, no dogs alerted on or around the doors where the scent containers had been placed. Lit mentions that the church had not been used for training prior to the test; therefore, any chance of prior contamination was eliminated.

Another possibility is that dogs were following other dogs and alerting to where other dogs salivated or otherwise left their presence: Lit doesn't believe that is correct either due to the difference in pattern alerts between marked and unmarked rooms, as well as the variation of alert locations in all rooms.

Lit concludes, "These findings confirm that handler beliefs affect working dog outcomes, and human indication of scent location affects the distribution of alerts more than dog interest in a particular location. These findings emphasize the importance of understanding both human and human–dog social cognitive factors in applied situations."

Where does cuing come from?

Cuing is not a new concept. Trainers at detection schools for HITS Training & Consulting have been teaching handlers how to prevent cuing for more than 20 years. To fix any problem in canine training, you must first figure out what the problem is and where it came from. *Cues* are verbal or non-verbal behavior by the handler that the dog has associated with its final response. Cues are taught to the dog during its initial training — specifically, a consistent behavior by the handler between the time the dog has detected the target odor and the dog's final response.

Some of those behaviors are intentionally done to train the dog; others are unintentional and are likely unknown to the handler. The intentional cues are faded away through proper conditioning. Trainers

■ Problems with cuing can be fixed, but they must first be recognized, and you must determine the genesis of the problem.

Chapter 22: Courtroom Testimony

and handlers who are not using a proper conditioning model, or who have not recognized potential cues in their behavior, may end up with a dog that relies on or is influenced by handler cues.

Through repetition, this cued behavior becomes part of the stimulus to the dog. To further explain, think of it as a mathematical equation:

$A + B = C$, where

$(A = \text{Target Odor}) + (B = \text{Handler Behavior}) = (C = \text{Final Response})$

If the dog relies on handler behavior to be part of the stimulus, several things can happen as follows:

1. The dog detects target odor and exhibits a behavior change recognized by the handler. The handler exhibits the cue (handler behavior), the dog recognizes the cue and executes the final response.
2. The dog detects the target odor and exhibits a behavior change not recognized by the handler. The handler does not exhibit the cue (handler behavior), the dog does not execute the final response and leaves the target odor.
3. The dog exhibits no behavior change. The handler exhibits the cue (handler behavior), which is recognized by the dog. The dog then executes the final response.

Our job as handlers and trainers is to eliminate the handler behavior so that the simple mathematical equation $(A = C)$ remains and thus supports our K9's reliability. Target odor and target odor alone is the stimulus for the final response. Our handler behavior should remain the same *after* reaching the target odor as it was *prior to* reaching the target odor so that no behavior of ours is used as a cue and learned by the dog. The handler does not change his or her behavior; the dog changes its behavior.

There are several exercises we can do during K9 training that will help us determine whether or not we have an issue with cuing. A controlled negative or blank training scenario is important to any training regime. *Controlled negatives* are exercises where no target odor is concealed in the search area. The handler must inspect the designated area and determine from the dog's lack of behavior change and final response that no target odor is present. The presence or absence of a target odor is unknown to the handler and the dog leaves the exercise without finding a target odor. If this is done correctly, we can conclude that the handler does not exhibit cues and the dog does not rely on handler behavior for its final response.

To take this exercise a step further, novel or distracter odors are concealed in the blank area. Again, that fact is unknown to the handler. After inspecting the area, the handler must determine from the dog's lack of behavior change and final response that no target odor is present. If that is done correctly, we can conclude that not only do the dog and handler not have a cuing issue, but also that the dog does not indicate on novel or distracter odors.

Both of those exercises should be done for varying amounts of time, from a few seconds to as long as 30 minutes. If documented correctly in your training records, those exercises can be used to illustrate your dog's reliability and credibility. To assist in your credibility and reliability, document all real-life uses/deployments with your dog, not just the times your dog indicates and drugs are found. Documenting each time during real-life deployments that your dog does not indicate/alert is important to proving your dog's reliability as it relates to the Clever Hans Effect.

As described in Lit's study, a handler's perceptions or beliefs can directly affect the working dog's outcome. When you deploy your dog in real life, you do so with the belief that drugs may be present. If that hunch or well-founded belief, based on various factors, were not present, the dog would not be used. With that in mind, each time you use your dog and no indication or alert is observed, no cuing issue is possible. Both your deployment and training log documentation can prove that the Clever Hans Effect has not affected your deployment.

The final part of Lit's study addresses handler credibility. A handler can cue or influence his or her dog to have a final response at a given time. We also could claim that the dog indicated when it did not. That is not a canine training issue, but rather one of police ethics and individual truthfulness. No amount of canine training could ever assuage such reprehensible police misconduct.

Chapter 22: Courtroom Testimony

Handlers must realize that some long-standing techniques and policies are not based in well-founded facts. Such policies and beliefs can set you up for failure when answering questions in court. The following series of questions attacks a long-standing belief that you should not reward your dog in a real-life deployment.
- "Isn't it true that consistent, ongoing training is necessary to ensure that your dog's abilities are still reliable?"
- "While watching this video, I noticed that you ran your dog past that window twice. Is it normal for you to check an area multiple times?"
- "When your dog responds, what does it normally do right before the 'sit?'"
- "When you were receiving your initial training and your dog responded with a 'sit,' when would you give the dog the reward toy?"
- "Was this a reinforcement of the correct behavior on the dog's part?"
- "In this video, you did not give the dog the toy until sometime afterward. Why was that?"
- "Didn't the dog's behavior or response mean that drugs were present?"
- "So when you reward the dog, that means you believe the dog to be correct?"
- "So when you didn't reward the dog right away, that meant that you were not sure if there was actually any drug odor present at that time?"

That line of questioning draws a big red circle around the belief that handlers should not reward the dog during a real-life deployment. If you believe in your training techniques and methodology, you should have complete confidence in the dog's reliability. If you do not reward the dog during real-life deployments because you are afraid of conditioning the dog to an odor outside of the target odors, you must evaluate this possibility against the need to reward the dog when it finds target odor during a real-life deployment.

Many times canine supervisors are called into court to substantiate the credibility of the canine training program. Supervisors may be asked to answer the following and many more questions.
- "Do you attend all canine training?"

K9s In the Courtroom

- "How do you know that your handlers and trainers are conducting training in a way that will create a reliable dog?"
- "What training have you attended involving drug detection canines?"
- "Explain how you can assure us that your handlers train as they should?"

When a canine unit supervisor is not or never was a handler, a defense attorney may try to exploit this portion of the unit. They are trying to show that the unit is not properly supervised and not following the training protocols set forth by the department in the detection canine training program and the policy and procedures manual, provided the agency has one. If a department hires a supervisor who has no canine experience, it should provide the supervisor with as much training as possible and be sure to have policy and procedures in place for the unit to follow. It is advisable to have a well-trained handler acting as trainer for the agency to provide expert experience and be sure the training follows all industrywide standards.

In this age of nonstop video of every portion of our lives, canine handlers should always operate with the belief that they are being recorded. Videos are widely used by defense attorneys and the experts they hire to punctuate any miscues or perceived errors by the handler. I will list the top 10 attacks to a K9 video by a defense attorney or their expert. These attacks are taken from a defense attorney seminar on how to defeat drug detection canines.

- The actual response of the dog sitting is way overrated. It is the actions of the handler and canine in the 10 to 20 seconds before that which are important.
- The canine should be showing "active sniffing behavior" and not just following along with the handler's hand presentations.
- The canine should be exploring and curious about areas other than the specific spots that the handler points out to it.
- The canine should not be looking at the handler constantly. This is a sign of a very dependent and unreliable canine. This is also an indication of a canine looking for some type of cue from the handler about where the dog is expected to respond.

Chapter 22: Courtroom Testimony

- Maintain fluid motions: handlers should keep moving without stuttering their step or hesitating when the canine is showing an interest in an area. Those actions on the part of the handler will become cues to the canine and cause a false or inaccurate response.
- Beware handlers doing a *tap back:* going back to an area where a canine has already checked and making them do it again. The canine will take this as a cue and respond even if nothing is there.
- The canine should be working almost independently of the handler and not actively paying much attention to him or her other than checking the presentation areas on occasion. A good canine needs little or no presentations from the handler. A good description of the handler's job is to do as little as possible and stay out of the canine's way. Handlers are merely portable toy or food dispensers for when the canine does it right.
- Once a canine responds, it should become a statue until it is given its reward. If a canine is seen to respond or "sit" and then immediately get back up again, that is a false response or a sign that the canine is weak in its task.
- If a canine does not get its reward in a timely manner, within 1 to 3 seconds, a good one will go back, sniff again and start getting antsy. A weak canine will get up and walk off.
- The handler should believe the canine the first time, whether it responds or not. If the canine responds and the handler has it check the area again, then rewards the response, that is a sign of a weak or poor handler who does not know how to read or trust his canine. In most cases, once a canine checks an area, the handler should not have it go back and check the area again. The only exception to this is if the handler recognizes that his canine is not actively searching, they may go back and do an area again.
- Wind direction is *critical!* Odor from drugs or whatever the dog is trained to find is heavier than air and will drop in low wind currents. This is the biggest issue in vehicle searches, large open buildings such as warehouses, or any other outdoor environment. For example, if it can be seen that the wind is blowing from left to right and the canine

responds to the door seam on the left side of the vehicle, but shows no interest on the right side, go back and look for cues from the handlers. The most probable spot for a response in that situation would be on the right side of the vehicle.

Detection canines have been and will always be the most critiqued and litigated of the canine disciplines. Handlers are likely to deploy their dogs for detection more than for any other reason. Training should reflect the abundant uses for detection and the critique that will follow. Records and training are not something you can go back and shore up after the fact. You must assume that you will be challenged in court for every deployment and train for that instance before it happens.

To properly defend your canine's indication from a defense attorney's attack, you must have good training and deployment records, use proper training techniques and methods, and be able to articulate those when testifying in court proceedings.

■ ■ ■

Index

aberrant behavior, 127–129
accidental bites, 27, 31–33, 42, 48–50, 56–57, 65, 97, 119, 124
adrenalin rush, 68–69
air support, 83,
    noted in reports, 88–89
annual recertification, 27–28
arrest team, 31, 70–71
    techniques, 71
attorney–client privileges, 101
audit, 55–56
backup officers (also, see cover officers), 23, 58
baton, 60, 68, 85
beanbag weapon, 59–60, 68, 82
bite equipment, 57–58
bite release, 53, 55–57, 91
blind search, 188
briefings,
    briefing training, 29, 31, 56–57, 114
    debriefing incidents, 76, 130
    noted in reports, 89
    pre-deployment, 70–71
burnout, 107, 110–114
call-off and re-direct, 61

CAnine Tactical School (CATS), 51, 57
certification,
    standards, 28, 37–38
    goals, 53
    lack of, 27
    recertification, 28, 96–97
    tracking, 122
    trainers', 37
    training for, 60, 80, 194
chemical agents, 59–60, 82
checkpoints (see narcotics-interdiction checkpoints)
civil litigation,
    settlements, 21–23, 25–26, 33, 49–50
    training to avoid, 50–51
Clever Hans, 202–203
Clever Hans Effect, 202–203, 208
consultants, 35
control hold, 68, 85
controlled negatives, 199, 207
courtroom demonstrations, 191–192
cover officers, 53–54, 62, 64, 70–71, 123–124, 130–131
creating a K9 unit, 34–47

Index

cues, cuing, 160, 188, 202–208, 210–212
curtilage, 147–151, 180
dead scent, 192, 200
decoys, 44–45, 61, 123
deployment, 49, 53, 57–61,
    after K9 announcements, 83–84
    avoiding errors, 62–76
    high-risk, 77
    litigation following, 21, 101, 126
    noted in reports, 86–87, 89
    post-deployment, 76, 87
    recordkeeping, 39
    recreating, 192
    successful, 127
    understanding limitations, 69
deposition, 47, 100–104, 106
    videotaping, 102–103
detection canines, 132–141
    certification of, 137, 140, 143–144
    odors, detection of, 141
    final responses of, 140
    general information, 139, 140
    medical records for, 140
    policies and procedures for, 136–138, 140
    recordkeeping for, 133–141, 144
    recordkeeping software for, 15, 54–55, 141
    reliability of, 142–146
    standards for, 38–39
    subpoena requests and requirements for, 135–141
    supervision of, 138–139
    training and certification for, 134–135
distraction device, 59
e-collar, 128
excessive force (see use of force)
external review, 33
Fair Labor Standards Act (FLSA), 93–95, 96
false claims, 26–27
false alert, 142–143, 194–195, 198
false negatives (see false alert)
Federal Statute 21 U.S.C.A §881(a), 166
field training officer (FTO) programs, 48
Fifth Amendment, 164
flash-bang devices, 60
forfeiture, 163–169
Fourth Amendment, 28, 70, 81, 86, 121, 147, 150–152, 154–155, 160, 170, 172–173, 175, 176, 179–182
gas mask (see safety equipment)
global contamination theory, 167–169
green dog, 43–44
gun dog, 183–189
    in article searches, 183–184
    in consent searches, 187–188
    in executing a search warrant, 184–187
    in gang or homicide search warrants, 186–187

in probation and parole sweeps, 188
in school searches, 188–189
handler compensation (see Fair Labor Standards Act)
HITS Training & Consulting, 13, 19, 206
in odor, 160
in-service training (see briefing training)
interrogatories, 18, 99–100
Koninklijke Nederlandse Politiehond Vereniging (KNPV), 43
K9 announcements, 18, 24–25, 70, 77–84
    content, 82–83
    noted in reports, 86, 90–92,
    mobile, 80–81
    legal issues in, 81–82, 96
    secondary, 79–80
    in tracking, 125, 127
K9 applications, 183–189
K9 behavior change, 202
K9 bite pictures, 18, 74–75, 88
    noted in reports, 92
K9 drives, 42
K9/handler mix, 32, 40
K9 handler selection, 40–42
K9 liability settlement agreement, 49–50
K9 policy (K9 manual), 18, 27–28, 38–40, 49, 96, 121, 136–138, 140
K9 public demonstrations, 30, 42
K9 selection, 42–44,

K9 socialization, 30, 42
K9 supervision, 18, 26–27, 31, 42, 45–47, 111–114
Kevlar helmet (see safety equipment)
knock-and-talk, 147
lawsuit preparation, 56, 96–106
legal cases:
    Albanese v. Bergen County, New Jersey, 94
    Andrews v. Dubois, 94
    Baker v. Stone County, Missouri, 95
    Brock v. City of Cincinnati, 95
    Bryan v. McPherson, 67
    Burrows v. City of Tulsa, 81
    Chew, 66
    City of Indianapolis v. Edmond, 153
    Crenshaw v. Lister, 82
    Cruz v. State, 162
    Deorle v. Rutherford, 66, 82
    Estate of Garcia v. City of Sacramento, 81
    Estate of Rodgers v. Smith, 82
    Evans v. City of Aberdeen, 168
    Florida v. Jardines, 147–152, 179, 182
    Florida v. Harris, 134, 141, 142–146, 198–199
    Franklin v. Foxworth, 66
    Graham v. Connor, 24, 66, 81, 86, 96, 121
    Gregory v. County of Maui, 67

Index

Haugen v. Brosseau, 66
Headwaters, 67
Hellmers v. Town of Vestal, New York, 95
Holzapfel v. Town of Newburgh, New York, 95
Howard v. City of Springfield, Illinois, 95
Jackson, 82
State of Kansas v. Brewer, 145
Karr v. City of Beaumont, Texas, 95
Kuha v. City of Minnetonka, 81
Kyllo, 182
Leever v. Carson City, Nevada, 95
Letner v. City of Oliver Springs, 95
Levering v. District of Columbia, 93–94
Lindo v. State, 170, 172
Mayhew v. Wells, 94
Nichols v. City of Chicago, 94
Noble v. State, 162
Omar v. State, 162
People v. $1,124.905 U.S. Currency and One 1988 Chevrolet Astrovan, 163
Reich v. New York City Transit Authority, 94
Rudolph v. Metropolitan Airports Commission, 94
Scott v. City of New York, 95

State Dept. of Hway Safety and Motor Vehicles v. Holguin, 163
State v. Logan, 162
State v. Nguyen, 152
State v. Washburn, 176, 179
Szabla v. City of Brooklyn Park, Minnesota, 81
Tennessee v. Garner, 66
Thomson v. Salt Lake County, 82
Trammell v. Thomason, 81
Treece v. City of Little Rock, Arkansas, 94
Truslow v. Spotsylvania County Sheriff, 94
Smith v. City of Hemet, 66, 68
United States v. Brooks, 150, 151
United States v. Burrows, 145
United States v. Dunn, 149, 151
United States v. Florez, 133
United States v. Hutchinson, 160
United States v. Lyons, 162
United States v. Martinez, 155–156
United States v. McCaster, 151
United States v. Scott, 151
United States v. Stone, 159
U.S. v. Brock, 179
U.S. v. Funds in the Amount of Thirty Thousand Six Hundred Seventy Dollars, 163, 165
U.S. v. Mathews, 150

U.S. v. Penaloza-Romero, 148
U.S. v. Parrilla, 180
U.S. v. Quoc Viet Hoang, 173
U.S. v. Venema, 179
Vathekan v. Prince George's County, MD, 81
Whren v. United States, 156
less-lethal tools (options), 59–60, 67–68, 97
lingering odor, 193
Lisa Lit, 203–206, 208
Lexipol, 38
maintenance training, 44, 50–51
mandatory rotation, 107–110
medically trained officers (see paramedics)
methyl benzoate, 168
motion of summary judgment (MSJ), 25
narcotics-interdiction checkpoints, 153–157
   real, 153–155
   fake, 155–157
National Police Canine Association (NPCA) 38, 51
non-compliant suspects (see passive suspects)
North American Police Work Dog Association (NAPWDA), 38, 51
obedience, 44, 55
Oskar Pfungst, 203
overwhelming force (also, see use of force), 59–60, 121
PACKTRACK, 54–55

paramedics, 24,
   legal issues, 96
   noted in reports, 88, 91
passive suspects, 60–61
Peacekeeper, 78
perimeters, 24–25, 56, 62–64, 70, 73, 78–81, 126
   noted in reports, 88–89
   setting up a search team, 69
   versus foot pursuits, 62–64
pepper spray, 68, 85
preponderance of the evidence, 163–164
primary purpose, 154–155
proofing, 195–196, 199
public address (PA) system, 79–81
   noted in reports, 89–90
recordkeeping, 18, 27, 34–35, 54–55, 61, 96, 115, 118–120, 131
report writing, 18, 85–92
   photographs in, 87–88, 92
review for deposition, 101
supervisory review, 47
request for production, 100
residual odor, 145–146, 200
safety equipment, 72, 128
scan, 191
scent-discriminate, 158
Schutzhund, 43
sniff warrant, 148
stale odor (see dead scent)
SWAT, 18, 40, 68–73, 78–80, 124, 130

Index

SWAT & K9s Interacting During Deployment School (SKIDDS), 51, 57
tactical deployments, 29, 52, 71–74
tactical scenarios, 29
    overwhelming force, 59–60
    training for, 29, 51
Tactical Operations for Patrol and SWAT, 24, 55
tactical vest (see safety equipment)
tap back, 211
target odors, 197–xx, 207–209
Taser, 59–60, 68, 85, 127
testifying, 104–105
testing documentation, 44
titled dog, 43–44
tracking, 115–131
    advanced training, 121–123
    control, 123–125, 127, 130
    recordkeeping, 121
    recordkeeping software for, 15, 54–55, 141
trainer selection, 35–38
training for the street, 18–19, 28–30, 52, 57–58, 212
    as you deploy, 80
    bite work, 119
    failure, 61, 130
    goals, 200–201
    maintenance, 50–51
    mistakes (see proofing), 195, 201–202
    recordkeeping software for, 15, 54–55, 141
    scenario-based, 129–131
training standards, 27–28, 34, 38, 51
    advanced training, 51–54
    recognizing burnout, 110–111
    lawsuit preparation, 96, 98
unit assessment (see audit)
United States Police Canine Association (USPCA), 38, 51
use of force, 24, 66–68, 82, 96, 131
    case law, 59
    complaints, 26, 41
    documenting, 85–86
    department policy, 101
    excessive, 26,
    overwhelming, 59–60
vendor selection, 35–36
Wilhelm von Osten, 202–203
wind-scenting, 116